This book in three words: exponential spiritual impact. Read and apply its message and it will impact your life, the lives of those you influence, and the many others whom they will, in turn, shape for Christ. *Organic Disciples* presents a biblical plan for changing yourself, your church, your community, and ultimately the world.

—**Mark Mittelberg,** executive director, Lee Strobel Center for
Evangelism and Applied Apologetics; author, *Contagious Faith*

I have long relied on the brilliant evangelism leadership of Kevin and Sherry Harney, and I could not be more thrilled for their newest contribution about holistically connecting discipleship and evangelism in the church today. This work is long overdue, and there is nothing out there quite like it. A must-have for your ministry library.

—**Michelle T. Sanchez,** executive minister, Make and
Deepen Disciples, Evangelical Covenant Church

In a world with so much confusion about what it means to be a disciple of Jesus, the Harneys not only shed light, they lay out biblical principles and practices that can lead us toward the life of fruitfulness we long for. So many have failed to see (and live into) the intimate connection between evangelism and discipleship. *Organic Disciples* fills this major void.

—**Kevin Palau,** president, Luis Palau Association

Kevin and Sherry Harney are some of the most genuine, faithful, faith-filled, and effective church leaders I know. I've had the privilege of seeing their hearts and the impact of their ministry firsthand. When they speak, I listen. They are a deep well of lived truth and grace. Let's all grow into more effective organic disciples by diving into this important new book together.

—**Craig Springer,** author, *How to Follow Jesus* and *How to Revive Evangelism*; executive director, Alpha USA

I love this book! It is one of the most inspiring and practically engaging books on discipleship that I have ever read. It is not about a formula or a system. Instead, it will stir your heart for more of Jesus and his love for people. The Harneys remind us that evangelism and discipleship never got a divorce. They are married and intended to work in union through the life of the believer and the church. The authors' braiding together of

prayer, worship, and Spirit-led action will compel you as you are going about your day to go and make disciples.

—**Nancy Grisham,** PhD, author, *Thriving*; former
faculty member, Wheaton College

Kevin and Sherry Harney love the Lord Jesus Christ and think strategically as force multipliers. *Organic Disciples* is carefully designed to effectively force multiply for the Lord Jesus Christ.

—**Lieutenant General Eric P. Wendt (retired),**
United States Army, Special Forces[*]

For the longest time, it seems that many in the church have pitted discipleship and evangelism against one another. For many churches, it does seem more emphasis is placed on discipleship to the neglect of evangelism. However, as Kevin and Sherry Harney rightly point out, the more Christians become like Jesus, the more they will engage in Jesus' mission. My hope and prayer is that the global church will embrace the biblical vision laid out in this book.

—**Josh Laxton,** PhD, codirector, Wheaton College Billy Graham
Center; co-regional director, Lausanne Movement North America

Organic Disciples offers a simple way to help your church raise up and multiply disciples. The seven markers provide helpful, clear language to assess where you and your church are in your discipleship journey, as well as identify opportunities to teach and grow. I love that this book, in addition to being theologically rooted and based on research with hundreds of churches and ministries, creates the bridge between discipleship and evangelism that is often missed. This book invites you not only to deepen your discipleship journey but also to be a disciple whose heart breaks for the people around them.

—**Eliza Cortés Bast,** pastor; Supervisor of Local Missional Engagement
and Strategic Ministry Initiatives, Reformed Church in America

---

[*] This endorsement is Lieutenant General (retired) Wendt's personal view and does not imply DoD, US Army, or US Army Special Forces endorsement.

As they did for evangelism with the Organic Outreach book series, Kevin and Sherry Harney bring practical application to discipleship as it was intended to be. *Organic Disciples* exposes the missing link between discipleship and evangelism, laying out a path that leads Christians through the one with the outcome of the other—exactly what Jesus demonstrated in the Bible.

—**Walt Bennett,** president, Organic Outreach International

I welcome how Kevin and Sherry reunite evangelism and discipleship, creating a natural, step-by-step approach to fulfilling the Great Commission. Using the stories of Jesus keeps the Bible as the textbook, while their personal stories make it practical. This book is incredibly valuable.

—**Anita Eastlack,** Executive Director of Church Multiplication, Wesleyan Church

I have known Kevin and Sherry for more than two decades, and I trust them to lead Christians deeper in discipleship and boldly into the world with the life-changing good news of Jesus. *Organic Disciples* will help you do both.

—**Lee Strobel,** author, *Case for Heaven* and the bestselling *The Case for Christ*

Organic
DISCIPLES

Other Books by Kevin and Sherry Harney

Organic
DISCIPLES

SEVEN WAYS TO GROW SPIRITUALLY
AND NATURALLY SHARE JESUS

Kevin G. Harney and Sherry Harney

ZONDERVAN
REFLECTIVE

ZONDERVAN REFLECTIVE

Organic Disciples
Copyright © 2021 by Kevin Harney and Sherry Harney

Requests for information should be addressed to:
Zondervan, *3900 Sparks Dr. SE, Grand Rapids, Michigan 49546*

Zondervan titles may be purchased in bulk for educational, business, fundraising, or sales promotional use. For information, please email SpecialMarkets@Zondervan.com.

ISBN 978-0-310-12015-5 (softcover)
ISBN 978-0-310-12016-2 (ebook)
ISBN 978-0-310-12017-9 (audio)

Cover design: RAM Creative
Cover photo: © Zen Chung / Pexels
Interior design: Denise Froehlich

Printed in the United States of America

21 22 23 24 25 /LSC/ 10 9 8 7 6 5 4 3 2 1

We dedicate this book to the hundreds of people who have taken our hands over the years and helped us climb upward on the journey of becoming more like Jesus. In large and small ways, you have shown us what it looks like to follow the Savior and you have taught us how to help others do the same.

The names are too many to list, but there are some who have invested years or decades in our spiritual journey. Some are still taking our hands to this day. Others are with the great host of witnesses cheering us on from heaven. For all of you we are eternally grateful.

I (Sherry) dedicate this book to all those who have significantly poured into my spiritual journey, including Sherwin and Joan Vliem, Larry and Marilyn Vliem, Chuck and Jean Van Engen, Elaine Garvelink, Alice Berry, Maria Nyitray, Lucille Patmos, Gayle Deur, Nancy Kreer, and Marilyn Hontz.

I (Kevin) dedicate this book to the men who have invested graciously in my life of faith through mentoring and discipling me, including Doug Drainville, Dan Webster, Jon Byron, Chuck Van Engen, Ron Geschwendt, Warren Burgess, John Schaal, Karl Overbeek, and Paul Cedar.

Contents

Acknowledgments

After more than thirty years of church ministry and writing, we have learned that everything is better when it is done in community. This book exists because of five important teams of people.

The first is a faithful group of servants who have ministered together at Shoreline Church in Monterey, California. This group of leaders has helped us develop, refine, and implement the seven markers of spiritual maturity. They are Walt Bennett, Greg Broom, Donna Brown, Nate Harney, Zach Harney, Danny Killough, Keith Krueger, Kim McDonald, Dennis McFadden, Roy Piña, Romel Retzlaff, Tyler Smith, Ben Spangler, Shawn Stroud, and Nate Tibbs. We also want to thank Jacob Perl for his work in the development of the seven spiritual marker icons. To each of you: your contribution has touched more lives than you know through the ministry of Shoreline Church and now through the kingdom impact of this book and all of its related resources.

The second team is the Organic Outreach International family. Walt Bennett, Tom Green, Robin Maguire, and their team of volunteers have been creative, passionate, and prayerful as they equip global leaders to share the gospel. Our international partners and leaders have helped us to understand how universal these concepts are across cultures: Steve Murray (New Zealand), Sudhir Mekala and Jayakumar Garnipudi (India), Che Ko and Va Bi (Myanmar),

David Okeyo (Kenya), Peter Rozghon (Ukraine), and other sacrificial church leaders. Two key pastors in the United States who have helped us try new things and continue to refine our work are Jeff Ludington and Ken Korver.

The third team is our amazing partners at Zondervan. It is staggering to think that we have been serving through publishing together for three decades. Ryan Pazdur, you are a friend, brother, and shining example of seeking excellence in all things for the glory of Jesus. Your wisdom and heart for the gospel have helped shape the message of this book. Brian Phipps, your attention to editorial detail inspires us and gives us confidence that the final product is always better than when you first laid your eyes on it. Steve Norman, thanks for editing and reviewing the manuscript with biblical integrity and the encouragement of a pastor's heart. Jesse Hillman and Alexis De Weese, thanks to both of you for helping us share the message of *Organic Disciples.*

The fourth group of people are denominational leaders and global influencers who have engaged in many conversations with us about the need for resources that bind together discipleship and evangelism. You have encouraged and challenged us to write this book, and we thank you for your partnership in the gospel. Some of these leaders are Mark Bane (Church of the Nazarene), Eliza Bast (Reformed Church in America), Anita Eastlack and Kim Gladden (Wesleyan Church), Wes and Claudia Dupin (Daybreak Church), Kevin Palau (Luis Palau Association), Craig Springer (Alpha USA), Michelle Sanchez (Evangelical Covenant Church), Ed Stetzer and Josh Laxton (Wheaton College Billy Graham Center), the board and leaders of Living Stones, New Zealand, and many others who have inspired us.

The fifth and final team is all of the people who have mentored and discipled us and invested in our spiritual lives through the years. Your names are too many to list, but your influence can be seen on almost every page of this book.

Preface

A Dream Birthed in God's Heart: Organic Disciples

Imagine a world where every person who follows Jesus is growing in spiritual maturity every single day. Picture neighborhoods, schools, workplaces, and every environment you enter influenced by Christians who love, pray for, and serve those who have not yet encountered the Savior.

Every Christian a passionate missionary right where they are.

Every school-age young believer praying faithfully for their friends to meet the Savior.

Every teenager who knows Jesus committed to loving their friends in the name of Jesus.

Every young married couple modeling faith and faithfulness to their coworkers, neighbors, friends, and children.

Every single person with a single pursuit: to shine the light of Jesus in a dark world.

Every empty nester leveraging their time and experience to bring the good news of the Savior to their next-door neighbor, to their family, and to the ends of the earth.

Every elderly Jesus-loving person so in love with the Savior that they feel compelled to share his story and faithfulness with the people they encounter.

The dream of God is shockingly simple, yet rarely realized. Sometimes the more Christians learn, grow, and engage in church activities, the less we move into the world with Jesus' love. For some, the more they learn about Jesus, the less they talk about him with people who are not yet his followers.

The dream of *Organic Disciples* is to help Christians mature in Jesus and shine his light in the world every step of the journey—for every believer, whatever their age or place of spiritual development, to carry God's grace, truth, and good news to the world. The closer we walk with Jesus, the closer we should walk with the lost in this world so that they, too, will experience the good news of Jesus the Messiah.

Foundations

Three Epic Questions

CHAPTER 1

How Can I Know I Am Growing as a Disciple?

How did we know we were growing when we were little kids? In my (Kevin's) home, it was simple. All we had to do was look at the writing on the wall. My family had a yearly tradition. Dad had us stand against the wall in the garage and he placed a ruler on top of our heads and made a mark on the wall. Next to the mark, he wrote our initials and the date. This tradition created a chronicle of our height. We could scan the wall and see how much each of us had grown from year to year.

We celebrated growth. If we had never changed, our parents would have been concerned. There was something wonderful about seeing, acknowledging, and rejoicing in the journey of growing up.

How do we know we are growing in spiritual maturity? How can we gauge whether we are taking steps forward in becoming like Jesus? Is it possible to see our character and lifestyles transformed by the presence and power of the Savior?

When we bear the name of Christ, we are on a journey to become more like Jesus. Our lifestyles, attitudes, motives, words, dreams, and goals are shaped by the ruler of the universe. When you think about it, this is a staggering reality!

How can we nurture this growth? What can we do to partner with God to become more like his beloved Son, Jesus?

Before we talk about spiritual practices that help us become like our Savior, we must look at our hearts. If we engage in all the right behaviors, but our character is nothing like Jesus, hypocrisy grips our lives. We are modern Pharisees who talk the talk and even walk the walk, but our hearts are far from Jesus.

The Fruit of the Spirit: An Umbrella over Spiritual Maturity

The fruit of the Spirit listed in Galatians 5:22–23 is not optional or exchangeable. Without the fruit of the Spirit growing in us, taking steps forward in spiritual maturity quickly becomes a legalistic exercise. If we read the Bible every day and study the Scriptures diligently so we can flaunt our knowledge or win arguments with nonbelievers, the discipline of Bible study will not grow us to be more like Jesus. It actually becomes repulsive to the Savior. Bible engagement, when it is not guided by the fruit of the Spirit, can damage our growth. In the same way, if we pray for the sake of impressing others, we look less like Jesus.

When our spiritual practices are superintended by the fruit of the Spirit, they shape us into our Lord's likeness. The fruit of the Spirit is like an umbrella over all of the markers of spiritual growth.

Love Joy Peace
Forbearance Kindness Goodness
Faithfulness Gentleness Self-control

Bible Engagement

Passionate Prayer

Wholehearted Worship

Humble Service

Joyful Generosity

Consistent Community

Organic Outreach

The nine fruits of the Spirit are about our character, and they govern our maturity process.

In the following sections of this book, we will dig deep into seven biblical markers of spiritual maturity. These are practices that every Christian needs to engage in regularly. Each one helps us become more like Jesus. They also propel us outward to the world with Jesus' love, grace, and truth. But if we jump right into the seven markers of spiritual maturity without addressing the need to grow in the character of our Savior, we might end up paving the way to radical legalism and paralyzing pride. Rather than becoming more like Jesus and drawing the world to the Savior, we could end up filled with spiritual arrogance, religious competition, and feelings of superiority. If the Spirit is not growing and guiding us, we could end up driving people away from the only hope of salvation.

Here are the nine biblical character traits that should guide our growth in spiritual maturity: "But the fruit of the Spirit is love, joy, peace, forbearance, kindness, goodness, faithfulness, gentleness and self-control. Against such things there is no law" (Gal. 5:22–23).

When the fruit of the Spirit blossoms in us, every aspect of our spiritual lives is strengthened. We will look at the seven markers of spiritual maturity later in this chapter, but we need the fruit of the Spirit for our journey. When the fruit of the Spirit is blossoming, Christian community is filled with gentleness and kindness. Service is offered with joy. Generosity is extended with a heart filled with peace and trust in the God who cares.

When we bear the name of Jesus and are known as Christians, we have the potential to lift up the Savior and make him known. We can live in a way that will draw people to the heart of God. But if we are known to be Christians and our character and lifestyles do not reflect the grace of Jesus, we give people an easy reason to reject the claims of the Savior.

We are his ambassadors. God's mouthpieces. The presence of Jesus in a world that desperately needs to see the face of the Savior. The truth is, none of us is the example we want to be. All of us fall short in our own strength. But in the infinite power of the Holy Spirit, we can grow to look, speak, think, feel, and live more like Jesus. In a dark world, even a little light shines brightly.

Spiritual Maturity Leads Us into the World with Jesus

Jesus has a passion for those who are lost. Every Christian was once a wandering sheep. Jesus came looking for us. We were lost, and then, amazing grace, we were found. Jesus' heart beats for those who have not yet understood his gospel and have not embraced his gift of salvation. The closer we walk with Jesus, the more our hearts will break for the lost and the more our lives will orient toward those who are still wandering.

If you think your spiritual maturity rests only on church attendance, biblical knowledge, and the occasional financial offering, there is much to be learned. Maturity is about looking more like Jesus, thinking like the Savior, feeling with his heart, and following his ways. Jesus' personal mission statement was to seek and save the lost. That's why he emptied himself and came to this world (Philippians 2; Mark 10:45).

Markers of Spiritual Maturity

In 2013 a team of leaders from Shoreline Church who minister to children, youth, young adults, couples, men, women, and seniors studied the Scriptures and discussed what biblical indicators help us to see whether a person is growing in faith. We longed to identify behaviors and practices that mark a growing Christian's life and apply to all ages and walks of life. We asked, "If we are growing as disciples, what markers should be apparent in our lives?"

With time, we refined our list and began sharing it with leaders around our community, nation, and the world. The response was strong. We landed on seven primary growth markers:

- *Bible Engagement:* learning to know, love, and follow the teaching of Scripture
- *Passionate Prayer:* increasing our ability to speak to God, listen for God, and seek God with others
- *Wholehearted Worship:* developing hearts, lips, and lives that celebrate the glory and goodness of God
- *Humble Service:* extending acts of kindness and service in the name of Jesus
- *Joyful Generosity:* recognizing that all we have is a gift from God and learning to freely share what we have
- *Consistent Community:* loving God's people and connecting with them regularly
- *Organic Outreach:* sharing the good news of Jesus in the flow of normal life

Developing each of these markers launches us forward in spiritual maturity. If we are to be fully engaged in growing to be like Jesus, we need all seven.[1]

A Recipe, Not a Menu

Restaurants are fun because we can look at the menu and choose what sounds delicious to us. At an Italian eatery, we can dine on spaghetti, ravioli, chicken marsala, seafood pasta, or some other dish that hits what our taste buds are longing for. There is something wonderful about picking what we love and avoiding things we don't enjoy.

But when it comes to spiritual maturity, God does not give us a menu to pick from. Our Creator wisely gives us a recipe for spiritual development. All seven markers are God's ingredients for growth. We cannot pick and choose among them.

When we're given a recipe, the idea is to follow it and include all of the ingredients. If you are making Grandma's famous chocolate chip cookies, but you use almonds rather than walnuts, and raisins instead of chocolate chips, you may be baking cookies, but you are not making Grandma's famous chocolate chip cookies.

When we are developing each of the seven markers, we move upward toward God, inward toward his family, and outward with the good news of Jesus. All through this book, you will see the intimate connection between discipleship (spiritual growth) and evangelism (reaching out with God's love). As you read each section, you will be challenged to worship God with fresh passion, grow deeper as a follower of Jesus, and share the good news of Jesus in new and natural ways. As this happens, you will grow. You won't see marks on the wall in the garage with your initials next to them. But you will see a growing love for God, an increasing engagement in practices that connect your heart to Jesus, and an ever-deepening partnership with the Holy Spirit to bring the gospel to a lost and broken world.

CHAPTER 2

Is Discipleship Bigger Than My Relationship with Jesus?

If we are traveling through this life alone, we are not on the journey Jesus has planned for us. Isolation and independence are not God's desire. Connection and interdependence are his passion. Why did Jesus spend so much time with the crowds, the Twelve, and the three (Peter, James, and John)? Why was Jesus quick to teach others? Could it be that discipleship is much bigger than our connecting with Jesus?

Every follower of our Lord who wants to grow in faith will walk through life locked hand in hand and heart to heart with other people. Community is God's design, and the richest faith is forged in relationship with others. We all need at least one Christian in our lives who is more mature than we are. This person can help us move forward with prayer, encouragement, challenging words, and exhortations.

Generation 1: We Need a Spiritual Mentor

 As a brand-new follower of Jesus, I (Kevin) was a student who was flunking out of high school. My GPA was 0.75. I grew up in a home with no Christian faith. No one invested in my spiritual growth. Intellectual atheism was the womb in which I was formed. This worldview can create a lonely life for a high schooler.

By God's grace, two really old guys (college students) took my hand and helped me forward. You can call it discipling, mentoring, befriending, or just helping me learn about Jesus. The term doesn't matter. What matters is that Doug and Glenn were guys I respected, and they invested time, care, and wisdom in me. They were kids themselves—both were fairly new believers just a few years older than me. But their care and friendship were a lifeline in my early journey with Jesus. They befriended me and began discipling me even before I was a follower of Jesus.

Today I have two godly men who still take my hand and help me grow. Each of them talks with me by phone regularly and keeps me accountable as a pastor, leader, husband, father, and neighbor. Karl Overbeek is a retired Reformed Church minister, and Paul Cedar is also a retired pastor who served as the leader of the Evangelical Free Church. I'm not fifteen years old anymore. I have been a pastor for more than three decades, and I am now a grandpa. But I still need people in my life who help me move forward in my journey of faith.

God has placed people in our lives who can take our hands and help us forward—if we let them. Like mountain climbers who know they have a better chance of making it to the summit if they climb with others, we should never travel alone. It is wise to have people in our lives who possess spiritual wisdom, who teach us, and who model what it looks like to walk with Jesus through life's joys and challenges.

Generation 2: We Are Responsible for Our Spiritual Growth

With one hand, we reach up and allow someone to help us forward and invest in our spiritual journey. But we do not expect that person to be the only one to keep us on track. As the fruit of the Spirit grows in us and we develop the seven markers of spiritual maturity, we are called to tend to our own journeys of faith.

In this book, we will look closely at these markers of spiritual maturity and learn how to take daily steps forward. With the fruit of the Spirit governing our growth process, we can ascend the pathway to becoming more like our Savior.

Generation 3: We Are Called to Invest in the Journeys of Others

With one hand, we connect with a mature Christian and invite God to use that person in our journey of spiritual growth. In addition, we take seriously our role in developing lifestyles and practices that help us grow in faith. But then, with our other hand, we reach back in the sacred role of discipling, mentoring, coaching, helping, or investing in the life of someone who is younger in the faith.

When we do this, they are blessed and strengthened. In addition, we grow as we help them learn God's Word, go deep in prayer, worship with fresh passion, find a place of service, learn to be generous, discover their place in the church, and share the life-changing story of Jesus.

This is a biblical picture of a Jesus follower: a person with one hand stretched upward and clasped to a believer who helps them grow in faith, and their other hand extended below and taking hold of someone who needs to mature in their faith. Do you see the picture? Can you envision these three beautiful generations of faith climbing together? Do you feel the excitement and glory of God that are unleashed as each believer is helped along in faith (discipled), takes responsibility for their own growth (being a disciple), and invests in another person (discipling)?

Shortly after I became a follower of Jesus, Doug and Glenn told me that I should be discipling someone else. Now, keep this in perspective. I was just sixteen and had been a Christian for less than a year. I was reading my Bible daily and learning to pray, and I was volunteering as a helper with the youth group at the church, but I was still very young in my faith. Nevertheless, God brought a young man along who was a year behind me in school and not yet a follower of Jesus. He was coming to the youth group and was pretty wild. I started doing what Doug and Glenn had done for me. I was a friend to him. I tried to be a model of Jesus to him. (In retrospect, my efforts seem a bit humorous.) I encouraged him to read the Bible and ask me questions. After five or six months, he became a follower of Jesus. His story was a roller-coaster ride of ups and downs.

This young new believer I was "discipling" had a brother who was a drug dealer and was teaching him the "family business." When this fresh, new high-school believer prayed to receive Jesus, he felt convicted that he should not be dealing drugs. He came to me and said, "Hey, I don't think I should be doing drugs anymore, but maybe I could sell what I still have and give the money to the church." He looked at me and sincerely asked, "What do you think?"

I just looked back at him and asked, "What do you think?"

He thought and said, "I think I should flush it all down the toilet!"

I affirmed his bold wisdom.

The next time I saw him, he looked like he had been in a fist-fight and had clearly lost. "What happened?"

He looked down, fighting back tears. "My brother beat me hard!" He explained that when his brother heard he had become a Christian and flushed the drugs down the toilet, he beat him up.

We talked, prayed, and I felt the presence of God's Spirit in that holy moment. I asked him, "If you knew your brother was going to beat you, would you still have flushed it all?"

He looked at me through tears and with an unflinching gaze firmly said, "I would do it again!"

I knew I was looking into the eyes of a disciple of Jesus. Only a few weeks into his journey of faith and he had taken up his cross, denied himself, and followed his Savior.

I was humbled and inspired to live more boldly for Jesus. Taking this guy's hand and helping him forward on his spiritual journey grew my faith. I learned that one of the joys of helping a person walk more faithfully with Jesus is that God inspires, challenges, and grows you. That has happened to me countless times over the years.

Four Generations of Discipleship

In one little verse, the apostle Paul presents a powerful picture of four generations of spiritual growth. Writing to his protege Timothy, he says, "And the things you have heard me say in the presence of many witnesses entrust to reliable people who will also be qualified to teach others" (2 Tim. 2:2). Let's call this the "2-2-2 Lifestyle." Here is the picture. Every follower of Jesus should be engaged with at least four generations of faith all the time:

- *Generation 1:* We invite or allow a more mature believer to help us grow in faith.
- *Generation 2:* We tend to our own journeys of faith and spiritual growth.
- *Generation 3:* We take the hand of a person who needs to grow in faith.

- *Generation 4:* We train and equip the generation 3 person to live this same way and to reach out to help someone else grow in their relationship with Jesus.

Can you see the four generations of discipleship as you read this verse? Read it slowly and let God clarify his vision for your life: "And the things you have heard me say in the presence of many witnesses entrust to reliable people who will also be qualified to teach others."

- *Generation 1:* Paul teaches and invests in Timothy, a young pastor.
- *Generation 2:* Timothy receives Paul's influence and grows as a Jesus follower.
- *Generation 3:* Timothy entrusts what he is learning to others who are reliable.
- *Generation 4:* Those reliable people teach others.

This chain of discipleship is powerful! It is world changing! It is God's plan for you and me and every follower of Jesus.

Generation 4: We Are Called to Invest in Others Who Will Follow Jesus

When Paul paints the picture of four generations of discipleship, the fourth generation is not meant to be the final one. It is a picture of continual spiritual influence from generation to generation until Jesus returns. As Timothy disciples others, he trains them to do the same. They take another hand and help the person below climb the summit of spiritual growth.

When followers of Jesus embrace this approach to life, growth will be unstoppable! You might ask, What can I teach another person? How can I be an example? What skills, lifestyle, and steps should I be engaged in? The seven main sections of this book will answer those questions.

The Beauty of Family Faith

My (Sherry's) journey has been quite different from Kevin's. I grew up in a family saturated with love for God, commitment to the church, and engagement in Jesus' mission. My parents, Sherwin and Joan Vliem, loved the Lord and sought to raise me in faith from the moment I was born. My parents served faithfully in our church. Both of them taught Sunday school for children and youth for many years. They didn't have a lot of money but gave joyfully and faithfully. They worshiped every Sunday and brought me and my siblings up to do the same. We had devotions as a family at the dinner table each evening. They modeled prayer throughout the day.

As Kevin and I began a family, I built on the foundation my parents had laid for me. They had discipled me all the years I lived in their home, and they continue to have a significant influence on my faith today. Kevin and I teamed up to do all we could to point our three sons toward Jesus. By God's grace, each of our sons came to follow Jesus in ways that fit their temperaments and personalities. Each one married a lovely Christian woman, and they are now serving Jesus in the places God has called them to.[2]

Kevin and I have the honor of investing in the lives of each of our sons (and now our daughters-in-law). We pray for them and with them. We talk about what we are learning from God's Word as we walk through life. They all know they can call on us for wisdom and perspective at any time.

Now I am a grandma, and the joy of watching our children teach their children to know and love Jesus is a delight beyond expression. My prayer is for our grandchildren to love and follow

God. In this crazy and uncertain world, I long for the next generation to build their lives on the solid rock of Jesus Christ.

Can you see the four generations of discipleship? My parents took my hand (and the hands of my brother, Mark, and sister, Dawn). They did all they could to help us grow up in faith. Today my sister, Dawn, and I walk with Jesus and seek to pass on the faith to the next generation. Our little brother, Mark (who stood six foot four inches tall), lost his battle with cancer but won the ultimate fight and is now with Jesus. His wife and two daughters are holding on to Jesus in their joys and times of sorrow.

Kevin and I took the hands of each of our sons (and now their wives), and they are all growing in faith. The fourth generation is now unfolding as our children have heard the call to disciple their children and do their best to lead them to the heart and arms of the Savior.

I love how this generational legacy of family faith is clearly painted in Psalm 78. Read these words and watch for four generations of discipleship:

> He decreed statutes for Jacob
> and established the law in Israel,
> which he commanded our ancestors
> to teach their children,
> so the next generation would know them,
> even the children yet to be born,
> and they in turn would tell their children.
> Then they would put their trust in God
> and would not forget his deeds
> but would keep his commands.
>
> —Psalm 78:5–7

What could happen if every Christian embraced this call? What if we all were growing in the fruit of the Spirit? What if each of us took a hand to help us grow, extended a hand to help another grow, and taught that person how to take the hand of someone else? What if we all were growing in the seven spiritual markers and helping others to do the same?

This is the dream of *Organic Disciples*. This is the desire of God's heart.

CHAPTER 3

What Is the Relationship between Discipleship and Evangelism?

After Jesus rose from the dead, victorious over the grave, hell, and the power of Satan, he gave his followers instructions. One of the final things he said is, "All authority in heaven and on earth has been given to me. Therefore go and make disciples of all nations, baptizing them in the name of the Father and of the Son and of the Holy Spirit, and teaching them to obey everything I have commanded you. And surely I am with you always, to the very end of the age" (Matt. 28:18–20).

With these words, Jesus lifted up both discipleship and evangelism, and he clarified their connection. Here is a helpful way to look at the relationship between these two lofty and important callings.

- Evangelism and discipleship are not enemies.
- Evangelism and discipleship are not just friends.
- Evangelism and discipleship are marriage partners.

To look at evangelism and discipleship as enemies is foolishness. When a church or pastor says, "We are really a discipleship church," and implies that they leave outreach to other churches, they are not following Jesus' command. We should never set discipleship and evangelism against each other. They are not at odds. It is just as dangerous to say that your church is all about evangelism and will not offer robust opportunities for believers to mature. This is to abdicate the heart of our mission to others. This does not please God either. Evangelism and discipleship are not enemies.

When we say that evangelism and discipleship are not just friends, we mean that friendship is not an intimate enough description of their relationship. Evangelism and discipleship are not buddies who hang out occasionally. They are not friends who grab a cup of coffee when they can find the time. The only image that captures the covenantal and spiritual connection between these two practices is marriage. Evangelism and discipleship are bound together in the heart of God. They are inseparable. We need to affirm this biblical vision and pursue it.

Of course, few believers and church leaders brazenly declare that they don't plan for meaningful outreach or believers' spiritual growth. But their practices often reveal a commitment to one over the other.

The future of the church requires leaders who recognize that true discipleship moves people out with the gospel. At the same time, evangelistic churches are always growing disciples and helping them to become more like the Savior. Evangelism and discipleship are marriage partners.

Connecting the Dots

As we move into the rest of this book, you will quickly see a rhythm in each of the seven main parts. Because discipleship is about becoming more like Jesus, we begin every part by looking at the Gospels and our Savior's practices. We will see that Jesus powerfully exemplifies spiritual maturity, as he should, because he was God with us. If you want a crystal-clear picture of Bible engagement, look at Jesus. Passionate prayer was perfected in the Son of God. Our Savior showed us that he is worthy of wholehearted worship. Jesus modeled humble service as he lived, washed feet, and died on a cross. No one who has ever walked on this earth has shown more joyful generosity than the Lamb of God, who came to give his life and take away the sins of the world. The one who is very God of very God and who exists eternally in perfect community with the Father and the Holy Spirit entered into consistent community with common fishermen, outcast women, religious leaders, and the irreligious. The living Word of God came to show us that organic outreach is something all of us can do.

If discipleship is all about taking daily steps toward being more like Jesus, we need a clear vision of our Savior and how he exhibited each of the markers of spiritual maturity. You will get that picture in the first chapter of the seven main parts of this book.

In the second chapter of each part, we will turn our attention to what it could look like if we followed our Savior's example. Since Jesus modeled each of these seven practices perfectly, we will look at our lives to see how we can take steps to become more like him. We will identify some of the obstacles that get in the way and learn how we can grow in each of the markers of maturity.

The third and final chapter in each of the seven main parts is all about how true spiritual growth propels us outward with the good news of Jesus. This completes the picture. In each area of spiritual maturity, we look at Jesus as our example, we learn to walk in his ways, and then we follow him into the world to share his love and grace. This is the journey of an organic disciple.

An Important Point of Clarity

Sometimes the best way to clarify what we mean by a term is to be precise about what we do not mean. When we use the term *discipleship*, we do not mean a rigid process in which one person has complete spiritual authority over the life of another person. Organic discipleship is far more dynamic. Discipleship happens every time one believer takes the hand of another and helps them move closer to Jesus. We can even disciple a person before they put faith in Jesus. Discipleship is broad and beautiful. Sometimes it is more formal and happens regularly over time. It also can be short term. To get a sense of what we mean, here are some examples of discipleship as we define it:

- When a parent takes time every evening to teach their child how to pray and reads them Bible stories, this is discipleship.
- When a Sunday school teacher prayerfully prepares a lesson every week and passionately presents biblical truth to a small group of kids, this is discipleship.
- When a college student invests in the life of a high school student and spends time with them one on one modeling prayer, love for God's Word, passionate worship, a lifestyle of generosity, and love for the lost, this is discipleship.
- When a pastor prepares a biblical sermon every week and preaches with passion and faithfulness to a body of believers, this is discipleship.
- When a committed Jesus follower builds an authentic relationship with a nonbeliever and prays for them, prays with them, shares things they are learning at church and in their reading of the Bible, this is discipleship.
- When a couple who has lost a son in a tragic accident begins a grief ministry birthed of their pain and loss, and sees dozens of Christians and also nonbelievers gather weekly to walk together on a journey of healing that is embedded in the teaching of Scripture, the presence of the Holy Spirit, and the love of Christian community, this is discipleship.
- When a person agrees to mentor a new believer and takes

them through a basic Bible study and spends time with them to answer questions, this is discipleship.

- When a Christian school teacher or homeschooling parent educates their children (and sometimes other children) in ways that graft Jesus onto every part of learning and life, this is discipleship.
- When a company owner or business leader shares their love for Jesus and Christian faith in words and actions over months and years, this is discipleship.
- When grandparents pray for and with their grandchildren, share stories of faith, and model what it means to follow Jesus in every area of life, this is discipleship.

The list could go on and on, but you get the picture. Discipleship is helping people draw closer to Jesus, and it can happen in countless ways. When we take someone's hand and guide them closer to Jesus, they are growing as a disciple.

The term *organic* means "natural." When something is done in a way that fits who we are and aligns with the way God has made us, it is organic. Organic discipleship is helping people become more like Jesus in the natural flow of life, in ways that fit who they are and who God has designed them to be.

A Wonderful Bonus

As a gift to you and your church, we have worked with a team of leaders at Shoreline Church, where we lead and serve and have developed a simple spiritual-growth self-assessment of the seven markers of spiritual maturity. There is a version for students and one for adults, and if you take fifteen minutes to prayerfully and thoughtfully answer the series of questions, you will get immediate feedback on how you are doing in each of the seven markers of maturity. You will also receive practical ideas for how you can take the next steps of spiritual growth. You can find the free assessment online, for both students and adults, at the following web pages:

- *Adult self-assessment:* https://OrganicOutreach.org/ OrganicDisciples/sgassessment/
- *Student self-assessment:* https://OrganicOutreach.org/ OrganicDisciples/sgassessment-students/

Don't just take the self-assessment by yourself. Invite the person who is influencing you spiritually to take it too. Talk about it with them. Then invite a person you are discipling to do the self-assessment, and the two of you can use this as a conversation starter. You can delight in areas of growth. And you can set goals in areas you each want to move forward in.

PART 1

Bible Engagement

*The Power of an Unchanging Message
in an Uncertain World*

The Bible is the Holy Spirit–breathed truth of heaven. Jesus is the living Word of God, and while he walked this earth, he loved the written Word. He knew it, quoted it, and let the Scriptures speak to him and through him. As his followers, we need to know the Scriptures, love them, and follow what they teach. As we do this, the world will see an unchanging message of truth in a world of radical uncertainty. God's Word will send us out on Jesus' mission and teach us how to live in the world so that the light of Jesus shines brightly.

CHAPTER 4

The Living Word Loved the Written Word

M eeting relatives for the first time can be an exciting adventure. Many years ago, we decided it was time for our three boys to meet their great-grandmother in her retirement home. Kevin had two grandmothers, one we called Granny and the other one we called Grandma. Granny was loving, generous, and fun—everything you think a wonderful grandmother should be. Grandma, on the other hand, did not have those endearing qualities. She had a difficult life, and while some people rise up in fires of adversity, this was not the case for Grandma. Nonetheless, because we lived near her for three years when we were first married, I (Sherry) made a point of developing a relationship with her. For the most part, I believed I had broken through some of her hard exterior and felt pretty good about how we were getting along.

On the day we introduced our boys to her, when we first walked into her room, we had agreed that I would approach her and do all the introductions. I bent over her bed and explained that these three excited little boys were her great-grandsons and they had flown all the way from Michigan to California to meet her face to face. While she was never what you would call a happy person, her immediate response caught me entirely off guard. She made a fist and swung it at me. She almost caught my chin, but I pulled back just in time. Then the great-grandmother of our three sons called me an unkind name. You should have seen the boys' eyes. Kevin asked me and the boys to step into the hallway so he could have a little chat with his grandma.

One of the staff members heard the commotion and came toward the boys to help them make sense of what had just happened. I soon realized that while her heart was kind, her efforts fell short of how we wanted our sons to process this moment. She started to explain that "old people just get that way. With time, they can become mean." Around that time, Kevin stepped into the hallway and overheard the caregiver's explanation of Grandma's poor behavior. He interrupted her. "No, boys," he said, "Grandma has always been kind of mean. I love my grandma, but I don't really have memories of her being very kind." Kevin explained to our sons that when people get older, most of the time they just become more of who they have been all of their lives. "If someone has been sweet and kind," he said, "time and the struggles of life normally make them kinder, and they can even become sweeter. What is on the inside grows with time."

Grandma had a tough life. She was aging, so we showed her compassion. But we wanted our boys to know that time and the pressures of life don't have to make us bitter or angry. We used this moment to teach our sons that who we are through life tends to come out as we draw near the end, for better or for worse.

This reality certainly proved true when Jesus came to the end of his life.

In His Darkest Moment, Scripture Poured from Jesus

As our Lord hung on a rugged wooden cross, fighting for each breath, drawing near the end of his life on this earth, he gasped these words: "My God, my God, why have you forsaken me?" (Matt. 27:46). As the crushing weight of our sin was laid on the spotless Lamb of God, in a moment of mind-numbing suffering, what was on Jesus' mind? What words were on his lips? What flowed out of him? Jesus prayed the Word of God. Psalm 22 is a prophetic messianic psalm inspired by the Holy Spirit almost a thousand years earlier. It was written by King David and was on the heart and lips of our Savior as he bore the punishment we deserved. As Jesus was being crushed, what flowed out of him was blood and Scripture.

Like the Lord we follow, we can turn our hearts to Scripture in times of loss, pain, abandonment, and sorrow. Jesus gives us a powerful picture of honest lament and authentic conversation with the Father. Meditating on and quoting Scripture in the darkest of moments was the pathway of Jesus, and it should be ours as well.

Jesus loved the written Word of God (the Old Testament Scriptures). He spoke the very words of God because he was God in flesh. In addition, Jesus is called the Word of God, the exact image and representation of God—God's perfect way of communicating himself to his creation (John 1:1). As you read the four accounts of Jesus' life (Matthew, Mark, Luke, and John), you discover that the Savior had a passionate love for the Scriptures and an intimate relationship with God's written Word.

Jesus Fulfilled the Scriptures

Over and over the gospel writers were inspired to point back to prophecy that spoke of the coming Messiah. They connected Jesus' incarnation, life, death, and resurrection to specific events so that all people could see that Jesus was the promised Savior of the world. Here is a small sample of how the gospel writers showed us that Jesus fulfilled Old Testament promises:

- The Messiah would be born in Bethlehem (Matt. 2:6).

- He would be called out of Egypt (Matt. 2:14–15).
- A light of heaven would enter a dark world (Matt. 4:15–17).
- The hope of the nations would come (Matt. 12:17–21).
- He would speak in parables (Matthew 13).
- He would come humbly on a donkey (Matt. 21:4–5).
- Everything written about him in the Prophets would be fulfilled (Luke 18:31).
- While Jesus was on the cross, they would divide his clothes, he would be thirsty, and not one of his bones would be broken (John 19:23–37).
- He must suffer and then rise on the third day (Luke 24:46).

Jesus' life was so closely bound with the Scriptures that he was the fulfillment of the prophecies and promises of the Old Testament.

Jesus Quoted the Old Testament in Theological Conversations

Along with being the fulfillment of Scripture, Jesus knew the words of the Old Testament. They were in his heart and on his lips. All through the accounts of the life of Jesus, our Savior spoke the words of the Old Testament. He knew their truth and authority.

When the religious leaders tried to test Jesus and trap him, they asked, "Which is the greatest commandment in the Law?" (Matt. 22:36). Jesus responded by quoting from the great creed of Israel: "Hear, O Israel: The LORD our God, the LORD is one. Love the LORD your God with all your heart and with all your soul and with all your strength" (Deut. 6:4–5). As Jesus continued in a rabbinical discussion about the Messiah, he asked the religious leaders what they believed. When they said the Messiah was the son of David, the ancient king of Israel, Jesus quoted from Psalm 110. This account is found in the first three gospels. As Jesus spoke with conviction about the hypocrisy of the Pharisees and the teachers of the law, he quoted the prophet Isaiah, saying, "These people honor me with their lips, but their hearts are far from me" (Mark 7:6, quoting Isa. 29:13). Jesus knew that Scripture had to be the final authority, so he kept it locked in his heart, alive in his mind, and often on his lips.

When people were confused about who he was, the Savior pointed them to the Old Testament to clarify their understanding. After speaking in parables that were prophetic and severe, Jesus looked at the teachers of the law and the chief priests and said, "The stone the builders rejected has become the cornerstone" (Luke 20:17, quoting Ps. 118:22). Jesus used the truth of God's Word to make it clear who he was, and the religious leaders got the message. When Jesus quoted this Scripture, they were ready to arrest him, because they knew he was speaking about them.

To Jesus, the words of the Old Testament were powerful, heavenly, and part of his normal daily conversations. As his followers who want to be like him, we should be ready with God's Word ever alive in our hearts. Even when people might not agree or might be offended, there is power in the Word of God. Like our Savior, we should speak the words of Scripture often and with confidence.

Jesus Knew the Power of Scripture in Spiritual Battles

In chapter 4 of both Matthew and Luke, we find Jesus in the wilderness being tempted by the devil. Three times the evil one tried to entice Jesus to dishonor the Father. In each of these encounters, Jesus responded with some of the most powerful words anyone can declare in the midst of spiritual warfare: "It is written!" Jesus quoted from the book of Deuteronomy all three times. That's right, Deuteronomy—a book many Christians find difficult to read, filled with laws and regulations for Israelite worship (Deut. 8:3; 6:16; 6:13). Yet Jesus put the Scriptures to good use in fighting his

enemy. In the midst of this spiritual brawl, Satan tried to manipulate Scripture and quote it back at Jesus. Bad idea! Jesus countered
with Scripture and the enemy turned and ran for the hills.

What an example for everyone who bears the name Christian.
Our Savior knew that Scripture is a powerful weapon against
the enemy. Jesus quoted the Bible when the enemy was near. So
should we.

Jesus Referred to Characters and Events in the Old Testament

In our world, some people refer to biblical stories and ideas without
even knowing it. "That person is a Good Samaritan" (Luke 10:25–
37). "Do unto others as you would have them do unto you" (Matt.
7:12). "Spare the rod, spoil the child" (Prov. 13:24). "Eat, drink, and
be merry" (Eccl. 8:15). "The writing is on the wall" (Dan. 5:5). All
of these phrases are drawn from the Bible.

Jesus made biblical references during the flow of normal conversations. Sometimes we don't even notice he is doing this. Jesus
talked about King David eating holy bread; helping a sheep out of a
pit on the Sabbath; a wicked generation that seeks a sign; the Ten
Commandments; the days of Noah; Elijah and the widow; Elisha
and the leper; the city of Nineveh; manna in the wilderness; and
many other stories and events from the Old Testament and the
history of Israel. It's amazing how often Jesus mentioned something
from the Scriptures during a conversation.

Jesus Upheld the Authority of the Bible

Throughout the history of the church, there have been those who
question the importance and authority of the Old Testament, casting doubt on the relevance or value of the first two-thirds of the
Bible. They celebrate the New Testament but don't seem as excited

about the Old. Yet Jesus affirmed the Holy Spirit–breathed truth of all the Scriptures, and at a time when the only Bible in existence was what we today call the Old Testament.

In the Sermon on the Mount, the most famous and important sermon ever preached, Jesus clarified his view of the Scriptures: "Do not think that I have come to abolish the Law or the Prophets; I have not come to abolish them but to fulfill them. For truly I tell you, until heaven and earth disappear, not the smallest letter, not the least stroke of a pen, will by any means disappear from the Law until everything is accomplished. Therefore anyone who sets aside one of the least of these commands and teaches others accordingly will be called least in the kingdom of heaven, but whoever practices and teaches these commands will be called great in the kingdom of heaven (Matt. 5:17–19). Our Lord never encouraged us to do away with the teaching of Moses or the prophetic writings. Rather, he came to fulfill what Moses and the prophets had written about and to make their teaching understandable. Our Savior helped people follow the teaching of Scripture, and he made it clear that every sentence, every word, and every letter of the Old Testament was to be cherished and embraced. Nothing was to be set aside or treated as a secondary or lesser authority.

Our Savior gave a stern warning and a word of blessing. Don't set aside or ignore any of the commands of God. If you do, prepare to be the least in the kingdom of heaven. But Jesus affirmed that those who hold to the commandments and teach others to do so will be called the greatest in the kingdom of heaven. As we follow Jesus the Messiah, we will learn to uplift the value of every word of the Bible.

Of course, we can't read the Old Testament (or the New Testament) simplistically. We need to understand the historical context. The Bible progressively reveals who God is, and so we read the Old Testament in light of the New and in the context of what Jesus has done. In fulfilling the law, Jesus also fulfilled the purpose of the ceremonial and civic laws that governed Israel. These are still examples to us of the character of God, when understood in context, but they aren't directly applicable to followers of Christ the way they were when God first gave them to his people. On the other hand, many of the Old Testament laws reveal truth that is timeless and more directly speaks to us today, revealing the unchanging character of the God who gave the law. Many of these laws are reaffirmed by the New Testament church.

The Bible will always be our authority. But we need to understand not only what it says but also what it means for the church and believers today. This comes as we study it closely, interpret it wisely, and follow it faithfully.

Jesus Corrected Warped Views of the Scriptures

In Jesus' day, many religious people in roles of leadership fancied themselves experts in all things related to God. They were called teachers of the law, Pharisees, Sadducees, and other titles. When Jesus encountered these people, he often had fiery conversations with them, disagreements about how to interpret the Bible. Jesus was quick to ask questions—often quicker to ask questions than he was to give answers. And he corrected those who were abusing and manipulating the Scriptures.

In one encounter with the Pharisees and the teachers of the law, Jesus called them out for letting their man-made traditions take precedence over the teaching of the Bible (Matt. 15:1–9). These leaders manipulated Scripture, wrapping it in the tradition they had created and attempting to hide their money in a legal loophole so they would not have to follow God's law and help their own parents in times of need. Their words parroted the Scriptures, but their hearts were out of line with God's will. Moments like this broke the Savior's heart and often angered him. He spoke the truth, calling people to align their lives with God's Word.

Many times Jesus said, "Have you never read . . .?" (Matt. 21:16, 42). He asked this to point out that people were not following the prophets or the Scriptures. It was as if they had not bothered reading God's revelation at all. Either they had not taken time to read the Scriptures, or they had not comprehended what God was teaching.

Jesus also confronted the religious leaders and plainly told these "Scripture experts," "You don't know the Scriptures" (Matt. 22:29; Mark 12:24). In the Gospel of John, Jesus told them that God's Word clearly points to the Messiah, and yet they completely missed the fact that the Messiah was standing right in front of them (John 5:39–40). Jesus corrected the Old Testament experts even when they might be offended.

Jesus Taught the Scriptures Every Chance He Had

All through the Gospels, we see Jesus teaching the Old Testament Scriptures. When you read the fast-paced Gospel of Mark (the shortest of the four accounts), you find Jesus teaching in a wide variety of settings:

- The formal setting of synagogue worship (Mark 1:21, 39; 6:2).
- In homes packed to the rafters with people (Mark 2:2).
- To his followers as they walked along (Mark 2:23–28).
- Before massive crowds (Mark 6:34).
- As he moved from village to village (Mark 6:6b).

Jesus loved to preach and teach and did it whenever he could. The Gospel of Luke tells us that teaching in the temple area became dangerous for Jesus because many of the religious leaders wanted to have him killed, yet despite the danger, "every day he was teaching at the temple" (Luke 19:47). The power of God's Word was so great and its truth so needed that Jesus kept preaching and teaching regardless of the consequences.

The next time you read the gospel accounts, take note every time Jesus says, "It is written." And pay special attention when Jesus begins a conversation or a time of teaching with the words, "You have heard that it was said." This is code for, "I'm about to teach or preach from the Old Testament Scriptures." As you pay attention to these clues, you will see Jesus' love for the Word of God. And the more you read the Gospels, the more you will realize that the living Word of God deeply loved the written Word of God.

And so should we.

CHAPTER 5

So Many Bibles, So Little Time

Kenton was a sophomore in high school when he became a follower of Jesus. He was high energy, a fun kid who came out of a secular family and a rough background. I (Kevin) was doing my best to lock hands with this young man and help him grow in the Christian faith, so I got him his first Bible and explained that it is God's truth from beginning to end. I encouraged him to dig in and promised him, "Kenton, if you make a reading plan and commit to learn from the Bible daily, I will read whatever you do so we can talk about it each week and learn together." He committed to read ten chapters a day (a bit more than I expected), and he followed through on that commitment.

Seven days and seventy chapters later, we had an amazing time talking and praying about what he was learning. There was a lot he did not understand, and he came to our meetings with many questions. There were also moments of deep conviction and encouragement as the Holy Spirit spoke to this young believer. For the next few weeks, and a couple hundred more chapters of the Bible, we read, met, talked, prayed, and delighted in the power and clarity of the Scriptures. Kenton was fired up, and his hunger for God's Word ignited my own faith and passion for Scripture.

The next time we met, all of this came to a screeching halt. Kenton had stopped reading the Bible. Not one single chapter since the last time we had met. I asked him why, and his response was both painful and refreshing. He said, "As I have been reading my Bible, I keep coming across passages that point out things I am doing that are wrong. I feel bad when I read these parts of the Bible. I don't want to stop doing these things. I enjoy them." He said, "I also keep reading passages that tell me to do some stuff I just don't want to start doing. So I stopped reading my Bible."

Wow! How honest can you be? This new follower was not complaining because he found the Bible irrelevant or difficult to understand. His problem was that it was too clear and convicting, so convicting it hurt to keep reading. God was showing Kenton behaviors that were wrong and needed to stop. The Holy Spirit was whispering to him about new behaviors and practices he needed to start. His response to this existential dilemma was to close his Bible, put it on a shelf, and refuse to read any more.

It actually made sense. Change is painful!

Love, Know, Follow

How do I know I am becoming more like the Savior? How can I be sure I am walking in his footsteps as a maturing disciple? One clear and powerful indicator is that I am growing to love, know, and follow the Scriptures with ever-increasing passion.[3]

Three elements to Bible engagement relate directly to our spiritual growth and maturity. First, we are to *love* God's Word. David, in Psalm 119:97, declares with confident boldness, "Oh, how I love your law! I meditate on it all day long." Psalm 119 is the longest chapter in the Bible, it is right near the middle, and it is all about the Bible. To love the written Word of God is good and right. It is Spirit-breathed truth and teaches us how to follow our Savior. Though we never worship the Bible, we should love it.

Second, to engage with Scripture means that we *know* what it says. It is not enough simply to have an emotional commitment to this heavenly book, to own a few copies (or a dozen), or to declare our commitment to Scripture's teaching. We need to feast on it, digest it, and let the words of the Bible form who we are.

Knowing snippets of the Bible is not true engagement. To grow as a follower of the Savior is to know the story of the Bible from beginning to end: The beauty and drama of Genesis. The oppression and freedom of Exodus. The sacrifice and worship of Leviticus. The heartache of the prophet Hosea. The tears of Jeremiah. The vision of Jesus painted by Isaiah. The conviction of God penned by Malachi. The theology of John. The story of the Spirit-saturated church recorded in Acts. The letters of the apostle Paul. The vision of Jesus painted in Hebrews. The apocalyptic drama of Revelation. Knowing each book of the Bible will form our faith and shape our lives.

Any Jesus follower who longs to grow strong in faith will embrace the practice of studying this staggeringly beautiful collection of sixty-six books written over centuries by vastly different people in varied contexts, yet all inspired by the Holy Spirit. Knowing the Bible is more than being able to regurgitate a few texts that inspire us. It's more than taking a few verses out of context and printing them on a plaque. It is knowing the whole story. Our Savior knew the Scriptures from beginning to end, and his followers should too.

The third aspect of this spiritual marker is that we *follow* the teaching of the Bible. Not only do we love God's Word and understand what it teaches, but we take action on what we learn. James puts it this way: "Do not merely listen to the word, and so deceive yourselves. Do what it says" (James 1:22). Our thinking, motives, dreams, and actions should be formed by this God-given book.

Every follower of Jesus will bump into biblical texts that rub them the wrong way. The high school student who believes in Jesus but "falls in love" and experiences the explosion of emotions and hormones that comes with a first romance will be confronted by the biblical call to holiness, sexual purity, and fidelity in a world that tempts them with sexual freedom and romantic ecstasy. College students who grew up loving and following Jesus will encounter professors bent on destroying their faith and undermining the Bible's teaching. Young people who read the Bible and believe it is true will be challenged to jettison their faith and adopt a more "rational" worldview. Adults of every age will find they live in a world that questions their biblical convictions and lifestyle.

Jesus' disciples need to navigate countless assaults on the Bible that our world, the devil, and our own rationalizing minds bring to challenge what we read and hear from God. We must learn to follow the teaching of the Scriptures in our daily lives even when our human wisdom resists. We must learn to amend our speech, attitudes, actions, and lifestyles to align with the teaching of the Bible, even when the world does not understand and we don't fully comprehend why.

So many Bibles, so little time (making a plan). It is possible for someone to be a new follower of Jesus and also be deeply immersed in the Scriptures. At the same time, a person can be a believer for decades, go to church faithfully, and yet not really know God's Word. The difference is deciding to dig deep into the Scriptures, read regularly, and have a plan for personal growth in God's Word. That plan can include using tools such as a one-year Bible-reading plan, a chronological Bible, an online plan, or one of dozens of other tools and resources.[4]

Knowing the big picture. In 2010 our church developed a one-day Bible experience titled The Big Picture of the Bible. In a single day, we taught our church the entire sweeping story of God's Word. We explained the Bible with eleven movements from beginning to end, from creation to consummation. Many people were able to make sense of the Bible for the first time. They had spent years, sometimes decades, bouncing around from verse to verse and chapter to chapter but had never learned how the entire Bible fits together. Once they understood the larger epic story, they could fit passages, characters, prophecies, and poetry into their proper place in God's story.[5]

During this season of ministry, we also took our church on a thirty-two-week chronological journey through the Bible called *The Story*.[6] Again, the entire congregation gained a new vantage point, seeing how the Bible fits together historically and chronologically. The Bible is organized by different genres, and the sixty-six books are not arranged based on a historical timeline. (This is particularly true of the Old Testament.) This makes it difficult for modern readers to grasp how it all fits together. For instance, the books making up the Wisdom Literature (Job, Psalms, Proverbs, Ecclesiastes, Song of Songs) are grouped together in the Bible, but these books span centuries of biblical history. The same is true of the Prophets, both major and minor.

Jesus followers need to know the storyline of Scripture. And when we do, the message of God's presence, power, love, mission, and redemptive plan takes on deeper meaning. And it makes a lot more sense!

From Snacking to Feasting

A "Bible snacker" is how we refer to someone who has one spiritual meal a week. They eat when they go to church and someone else is feeding them, but that's all they eat. This person is heading for spiritual malnourishment. No matter how good a sermon might be, it is not enough to sustain spiritual health. Followers of Jesus who long for spiritual vitality should be regularly feeding on God's Word. We find strength and power as we consume Scripture every day, sometimes more than once a day. Reading God's Word in the morning, as we begin our day, sets the tone and trajectory of our thinking. Using spare time to memorize and meditate on the words of the Bible while driving, waiting in line, or taking a break at work recalibrates our attitudes and thought processes. Reading and reflecting on a chapter in Psalms or Proverbs as we wind down at the end of our day and get ready for bed gives us peace and perspective. Think about this: what is the better way to finish your day—drooling on your phone or tablet after falling asleep in the middle of a show, or peacefully dozing off with God's Word in your hand, mind, and heart?

Hooks in your brain. Georgia was a great Bible teacher and mentor of children. She had a unique way of communicating the truths found in God's Word. One day, while teaching a complex biblical concept, Georgia said, "If this does not make sense to you right now, just put it on a hook in the back of your brain and leave it there. Don't forget about it, but don't worry about it either. When the time is right, you can take the idea off the hook, look at it, and think and pray about it more." She explained that God's mind and heart are so big that we can't fully understand everything he teaches in the Bible. As a matter of fact, we should not expect to. She finished by saying, "Even if it does not make sense for a long time, you can ask Jesus about it when you get to heaven." This is great Bible advice for kids *and* adults.

Information and transformation. It is easy for many of us to become knowledge junkies, growing obsessed with learning more and more Bible information. Of course, there is nothing wrong with studying the Bible and knowing lots of things about the text of Scripture, the context, and the meaning to its original readers. All of this is healthy and good. But there is a danger that gaining knowledge and knowing facts becomes the end. We begin to love the information we gather for its own sake, and we don't experience transformation. Something is out of balance.

Bible engagement and knowledge of the Scriptures should lead to transformed lives. Our thinking changes. Compassion grows. Humble service flows. Grace, amazing and free, pours from us to others. Holiness becomes our vision. The conviction of biblical truth should pierce our souls long before we run to share a powerful biblical text with someone else.

Exegesis or eisegesis? There are two primary ways to read the Bible. The first is to let the message, truth, and meaning come out of the biblical text. Theologians call this *exegesis*. The goal of a disciple of Jesus is to do all we can to invite the Holy Spirit to speak to our hearts, minds, and lives. We follow what God teaches in his Word. Even when it is challenging or rubs against our preferences or preconceived notions, we are called to adjust our lives to the teaching of the Bible.

The second way some people read the Scriptures is to impose their opinions, desires, and preconceived notions on the text. We decide what we believe or what we want the Bible to say and then search for fragments of the Bible (usually out of context) that agree with us. We decide on our opinion on an issue and then manipulate the Bible to line up with what we think. Theologians call this *eisegesis*. This approach is a dangerous form of spiritual malpractice.

The pathway of a disciple is to decide never to force our likes, tastes, or sinful practices on the Bible. Rather, we submit to what God clearly teaches in his Word. If our opinions and God's Word are in conflict, a disciple bends the knee to Jesus and adjusts his or her lifestyle to God's will revealed in the Bible.

Distracted or diligent? Do I spend more time watching shows on streaming services like Netflix, Amazon, and Hulu than feasting on the Word of God? Do I know the characters in my favorite comedy or drama better than I know the lives and teachings of Elisha, Esther, Malachi, Mary, Stephen, and Peter? How much time do I spend on digital games or social media compared with the time I invest each day encountering God through the Spirit-breathed Scriptures? Am I distracted by the endless options for entertainment that our world makes so easily accessible?

If I am easily distracted, I need to make a plan, establish a schedule to form a habit, and find an accountability partner. Bible engagement is the first of the seven markers of spiritual maturity we are considering. And we put it first because all of the other markers are built on this one. If we did not have the Bible, we would not clearly know how to become more like Jesus. If we don't learn to feast on Scripture, we will never learn the pathway our Savior wants us to walk.

4 Generation Challenge (2-2-2)

Personal Bible study should be part of our lives and a delight for every follower of Jesus. Organic disciples not only study the Bible but, as we saw earlier, follow 2 Timothy 2:2 and lock hands with others to learn and live the Scriptures in community. There are countless ways to do this, but here are a couple of ideas to get the creative juices flowing.

Beyond the "Popeye syndrome." In 1919 E. C. Segar created a cartoon character named Popeye the Sailor Man. This comic strip and character have now been around for more than one hundred years. Popeye was a unique "superhero" who gained his strength from eating spinach. When he opened a can of this dark green vegetable and popped it into his mouth, he was unstoppable. The cartoon was both fun for kids and a great way for parents to get their children to eat vegetables at dinner time.

Now, the idea that eating a single can of spinach will make a person immediately superstrong is absurd. But that's often how we approach our engagement with God's Word. It's equally absurd for us to think that a quick snack of Scripture will empower us to stand strong for Jesus against the forces of hell, our challenging world, and our sinful proclivities. Physical strength comes from healthy eating day after day, meal after meal, for months on end. In the same way, spiritual maturity and stability come as we read, study, embrace, and follow God's Word day after day, week after week, month after month, and year after year.

If you are locking hands with someone to spiritually influence them (or you are being influenced by them), you both need to be digging into the Scriptures daily and keeping each other accountable. Talk about what you are learning and how it is impacting your life. Share where the Holy Spirit is convicting or encouraging you. Ask questions that take you deeper into the text. Share your personal applications with each other and invite prayer and accountability. As the months and years pass, this will lead to growth in your lives.[7]

Memorizing and internalizing the Scriptures. As a child, I (Sherry) was discipled by both of my parents. They helped me progress in all seven of the spiritual growth markers. I first started to memorize Bible verses in Sunday school, and I have fond memories of the creative ways our vacation Bible school teachers helped us memorize verses. I remember when my dad decided he would commit the entire book of Second Peter to memory. Even though he wasn't confident he could do it, he wanted to try. Over the course of more than a year, he immersed himself in this New Testament book. It became so much a part of him that it overflowed into his heart, his mind, and many of his conversations. It was inspiring for me, as his daughter, to see him memorizing Scripture. And he encouraged me by his example to do the same.

While Kevin and I were raising our boys, we tried to offer them a similar lifestyle of Bible memorization, meditation, and internalization. Our boys now tell me that they remember me standing by the kitchen sink with a written verse on the counter trying to memorize or meditate as I washed dishes. To this day, there are always at least one or two passages taped up on the wall where I exercise and work on my Bible memory verses.

My parents and church leaders took my hand when I was young and led me in Bible memorization, and then I embraced this discipline on my own. Now I continue to encourage my sons and daughters-in-law with the hope that they will encourage others through their witness and influence.

There was a season when our oldest son and his wife were in a time of transition. As they prepared to make a move across the country, they lived with us for a few months. During this time, we were thrilled to have our friend John Grooters visit. John is a movie producer, and he gave us a copy of his latest film. One evening, my daughter-in-law Christine and I decided to watch the movie. It was titled *Tortured for Christ,* and it was sobering. It relates the story of Richard Wurmbrand, a Romanian pastor who stood for his faith and the gospel as communism was spreading across his country and destroying churches.

When Wurmbrand realized there was a high probability he would end up spending a significant amount of time in prison, he memorized one Bible verse for every day of the year. Richard had figured out there are 366 verses in the Bible that instruct us not to fear. On the day he was arrested, he asked one question: "What is the date?" He did not explain why at the time, but on that day, he began meditating on the first of the 366 passages he had memorized for this moment. The verse was Psalm 56:3: "When I am afraid, I put my trust in you."

This bold and faithful pastor experienced firsthand the value of memorizing Scripture, and this practice strengthened him during difficult times of suffering and persecution. Altogether, Wurmbrand spent fourteen years in prison. He was not allowed to have a Bible, but he carried the Word of God with him in his heart and mind. Though they tortured him regularly and demanded he reject his faith, Wurmbrand refused. His oppressors did all they could to force him to give them names of other Christians, but he would not. And when he was finally released, he began a ministry that continues serving the persecuted underground church to this day called the Voice of the Martyrs.[8]

After Christine and I watched this powerful movie, we decided to begin a journey of memorizing the Bible together. We felt it was best for us to start with one verse per week. We have been doing this for more than two years now. In the past, we were able to work on it together in person, but since we no longer live near each other, we simply recite our verses over the phone or on FaceTime.

The practice of memorizing Scripture continues to be a great blessing in my life. My parents and church leaders modeled and taught me the value of Scripture memorization. I took this into my heart and adopted it as part of my life. And I was able to take my daughter-in-law's hand and spend time doing Bible memorization with her. Soon, what we have done will impact a fourth generation as she shares this practice with her own family and others. Can you see the joy of discipleship over the generations?

The Rest of the Story

You might be wondering what happened to Kenton, that high school student who quit reading the Bible when he discovered that some of the truth he was learning made him uncomfortable. After I (Kevin) talked with him about the reality that Scripture can convict and challenge us, we discussed how God's Word protects us and guides us to live as God has designed us to live. We talked about how God's Word shows us the good path to walk, even when we don't feel ready to take the next step. Kenton decided he would get back to reading the Bible daily and do his best to follow what he was learning. His passion grew as he began reading again, working up to several chapters a day. Though I was discipling Kenton, his rapid growth and diligence moved me to read even more Scripture, and both of us grew in the process. What a joy it is to lock hands with others and walk in community as we grow in Bible engagement!

CHAPTER 6

The World Needs Good News

I (Kevin) was having lunch with my friend Ed Stetzer, talking about an upcoming conference sponsored by the Wheaton College Billy Graham Center. I was planning to say something during my presentation at the conference, but I wanted to run it by Ed first. Ed is a leading thinker in global missiology, and even better, he is direct and blunt, much like I am. I knew he would give me his honest opinion.

Here is the statement I planned to make: "Many people seem to believe that if we can get Christians to grow deep in spiritual maturity, they will naturally and spontaneously start sharing their faith with people who are not yet Christians. All evidence is to the contrary!"

Ed listened and we had a thoughtful conversation about this for most of our lunch. We talked about how becoming more like Jesus should propel believers into the world with the good news of our Savior. We dreamed of the impact that could be made if every Christian who was growing deeper as a disciple was also becoming more equipped to articulate their faith and the message of salvation. We discussed ways to help connect discipleship to evangelism so that every maturing Jesus follower increases in their commitment to shine the light of the Savior.

But we also agreed that, sadly, there seems to be a massive spiritual disconnect. Ed and I discussed the reality that many people who are growing in their knowledge of the Bible, attending church regularly, and seeking to increase their intimacy with Jesus are not joining in his mission to seek and save the lost. Though there should be a link, in much of the discipleship that happens in the church today, there does not seem to be a relationship between spiritual maturity (at least how it is defined by many today) and evangelistic activity. Instead there is plenty of evidence that the longer a person follows Jesus, the more disconnected they become from the world and the people Jesus came to save.

That conversation was one of the factors that led to the writing of this book. Sherry and I believe that growing closer to Jesus should move a Christian outward toward the world. Walking intimately with Jesus should move our footsteps where Jesus goes—to the broken, hurting, lost, and wandering sheep who need the Good Shepherd.[9]

The more we love, read, and follow the Bible, the more we should be moved to share our faith with others in organic ways. Attending Bible studies, listening to sermons, and reading our Bibles should propel us outward to the lost.

Our World Longs for Good News

Every generation has its share of bad news. This will never change. What has changed is the way we receive news and the endless barrage of bad news that hits us moment by moment. If we have a phone, we carry a powerful device that fires round after round of bad news into our pockets and purses. We get local, national, and global bad news delivered twenty-four hours a day. It can leave us feeling discouraged and depressed.

Good news is desperately needed. Unfortunately, the gatekeepers who decide what qualifies as news do not seem very interested in sharing stories that are positive, hopeful, and life giving.

The domain of good news, for the most part, has been left to the church. It is time to step in to share what the world longs to receive, because the Bible is loaded with good news. *Gospel*, the message of Jesus, literally means "good news." We have daily stories of God's grace, presence, power, and goodness that we can share. Followers of Jesus who feast on the teaching of the Bible and get that message deep in their souls will hear the calling of the Holy Spirit to share this amazing news with those who have not yet met the Savior.

Immersing ourselves in the Scriptures fuses the mission of God to our souls. A mentor of ours, Dr. Charles Van Engen, wrote a powerful book as part of his doctoral dissertation.[10] The title, *God's Missionary People*, reveals the aim of the book. Dr. Van Engen believes that when Christians look closely at the Scriptures and follow the Savior, we will see ourselves as missionaries. When we see the face of Jesus and are captured by his heart, our lives will naturally turn outward toward the lost. Every day becomes an opportunity to shine the light of Jesus and share his gospel.

When we view our Creator as the Bible reveals him, as a missionary God, we long to be like the one whose name we bear. This means we will be on mission at all times, in all places. Even as Jesus willingly left the glory of heaven and emptied himself, we, too, will set aside our likes, desires, comfort, preferences, and dreams. In the name of Jesus, we will bring his good news to a lost, hurting, broken, and hungry world.

Some people treat the Old and New Testaments like they are radically different messages. There are even those who avoid the first two-thirds of the Bible because they don't understand how it syncs with the last third. The truth is, both the Old and New Testaments are inspired by the same God, tell different aspects of the same story, and are saturated with the missionary heart of the Almighty. Every theme you find in the New Testament begins in the Old. Every message proclaimed in the Old Testament culminates in the New. From the first words of the Old Testament—"In the beginning God . . ."—to the final images in the vision of Revelation, we see the heart of our God.

The God of the Bible is loving to the core. He is holy through and through. God is present and engaged. Our God loves the world he made and the people in it (John 3:16). When Adam and Eve rebelled and turned from his will and presence, God's redemptive plan began.

When a follower of Jesus takes Bible engagement seriously and dives deep into the Scriptures, the message of the gospel comes through again and again. The scarlet thread of redemption is woven throughout this book, from the opening chapters of Genesis when God sacrificed an animal and made coverings for the nakedness of his children, to the Passover lamb, to the cross of Jesus. From Abraham's call to be a conduit of God's blessing to all the peoples on the earth (Gen. 12:1–3) to Jesus' commissioning his followers to make disciples of all nations (Matt. 28:19–20), the heart of God is unwavering.

When we fill our minds and hearts with the truth of the Bible, we will ignite a gospel fire that burns in our souls. We will love the nations with the passion of the Father. We will share good news by the leading of the Holy Spirit. We will follow in the footsteps of the Savior, who denied himself, took up the cross, and walked into a dark world, illuminating it with truth and hope.

The biblical narrative invites us into God's search for the lost. The God of the Bible is never passive. He is always on the move. When Adam and Eve rebelled and fell from grace, God came looking for them. When they hid, he searched for them. As they cowered, he cried out, "Where are you?" (Gen. 3:9). When they were naked, he clothed them (Gen. 3:21). When our first parents stood on the edge of another failure, God watched over them (Gen. 3:22–24). From the start, God protected the children he loved.

When a perfect and infinite payment for sin needed to be

offered, God took action. Jesus, the second person of the Trinity, left the glory of heaven and took on human flesh. He emptied himself (Phil. 2:7) and came as one of us so he could bear our sin, shame, and judgment. As Jesus walked on this earth, he invited his followers into his mission. Common fishermen made a career shift from fishing for carp and tilapia to fishing for women and men. He sent his disciples to preach the good news of the kingdom of God and reveal the power of the Spirit. Jesus was a man of action, and he called his people to join him in sharing good news with the world.

When Jesus articulated his personal mission statement, he put it this way: "For even the Son of Man did not come to be served, but to serve, and to give his life as a ransom for many" (Mark 10:45). Jesus came with the singular purpose of seeking and saving lost people—at the cost of his own life.

When the Savior died on the cross, he battled the forces of hell, Satan, and evil. He made sinful people righteous as he became sin for our sakes (2 Cor. 5:21). When he rose, the victory was won and sin was defeated. The dividing curtain between God and people was torn from top to bottom, and access to the very presence of God was opened for anyone who comes through faith in Jesus (Matt. 27:51). The entire message of the Bible centers on the redemptive plan of God's reaching out to lost people and making a way for them to come home. When this message takes root in the heart of a Jesus follower, we are compelled to join God in his commitment to seek and save the lost.

The Scriptures paint a picture of God's love for every person. We live in a world that divides people with growing precision. This process of treating people as if their group identities, genetic makeups, and personal backgrounds are of paramount importance creates wedges, not unity. If we are not careful, prejudice and preference will capture our hearts and move us to treat some people better than others based on these peripheral distinctions.

In God's heart, there are only two kinds of people. There are those whom God loves and delights in because they have come to him through faith in Jesus. And there are those God loves who have not yet come home to him. That's it!

When we read the Bible, we discover that our heavenly Father loves his creation and longs that no one would perish but that every human being would be saved by placing their faith in Jesus (2 Peter 3:9). In the very beginning, we see that God made human beings in his own image and longed for this good creation to stay in relationship with him (Gen. 1:27, 31). When Jesus walked on this earth, we are reminded that "God so loved the world that he gave his one and only Son, that whoever believes in him shall not perish but have eternal life" (John 3:16). Salvation is not universal, but the love of God and the offer of salvation are.

A serious student of the Bible will see the love of God all through the Old and New Testaments. What should amaze us as we read the Bible is not that God judges sin but that he offers grace so freely. God's patience is baffling. His kindness is magnetic. His love is astounding. His grace is still amazing.

The truth of the Bible awakens us to eternal realities. Heaven is real, and so is hell. This world will come to an end, and every human being will spend eternity either in the glory of God's presence or separated from his beauty and goodness (Matt. 25:46; John 3:36; 5:24, 28–29; Rom. 2:6–8). When we read the Bible, we are reminded that God is a perfect and righteous judge (2 Tim. 4:1, 8) and that he will make all things right at the end of time.[11]

For centuries, Christians were moved to reach out and share their faith with people they loved because they did not want to see them lost eternally. Believers risked relational conflict or the loss of a friendship because they accepted the biblical teaching that hell is real and that real people go there if they are not saved by Jesus. Today many churchgoers have adopted a soft or overt universalism that creates the false hope that every person will one day end up in heaven. This wrongminded notion can be embraced and maintained only by people who ignore clear biblical teaching or avoid the Bible altogether.

When we don't read the Bible consistently and closely, we miss the glory, beauty, and hope of eternal life that is painted with clarity in the Scriptures (Heb. 11:10, 16; Rev. 21:21). If we allow our eyes to be focused on the sparkly and shiny distractions of this world, we may forget that this life is a mist that will pass. As C. S. Lewis portrays in his brilliant book about hell and heaven, *The Great Divorce*, heaven is more solid, tangible, beautiful, and real than anything we will ever experience in this world.

As we read the Bible and take it seriously, we face the sobering reality that hell is real. We also embrace the joyful truth that heaven is offered to anyone who receives the gift of grace offered by Jesus the Messiah. Both of these will move us to bolder prayer for the lost, closer proximity to our neighbors, and more consistent sharing of God's message of salvation, the good news of Jesus.

Following God's Word, We Are Lights in the Darkness

Christians who love the Scriptures, who read the Bible consistently, and who follow what it teaches stand out from others in wonderful ways, and this often opens doors for spiritual conversations. Believers who follow the way of Jesus and the teaching of the Word of God look different.

In a self-serving world, biblical Christians serve humbly. We will dig more deeply into this topic in part 4 of this book, but when we read the Bible, we discover that our Lord cared for the hurting, washed people's feet, and offered his life on a cross for undeserving enemies. Then he called us to live like him. Christians are compelled to serve others sacrificially, and this lifestyle stands out today. When we see an opportunity to help someone, and there is no earthly reward or payoff, we offer to help. When someone asks,

"Why would you do that?" we can talk with them about the one who served us to the point of bearing a cross and giving his life. Biblical living naturally leads to spiritual conversations.

Followers of Jesus will stand out as we forgive others like Jesus forgave us. Over and over the Scriptures call Jesus' followers to extend gracious forgiveness. Jesus himself emphasized this as he taught his disciples how to pray (Matt. 6:5–14). The message of grace and the clear teaching that we have been forgiven saturate the pages of the Bible. Each time we extend forgiveness, we reveal the presence of Jesus. When we treat a person who has wronged us in ways that reflect the Savior's heart, it is a piercing light in a dark and unforgiving world. When others retaliate, Christians follow Jesus on the path of forgiveness and love. This opens the door to healing in relationships and creates a place for sharing about the Savior, who bore our shame, took our judgment, and forgave us.

We shine Jesus' light when joy flows from our hearts, even in hard times. One of the most beautiful examples of joy leading to evangelism is found in Acts 16. Paul and Silas had been stripped, beaten with rods, and publicly flogged. After this, they were thrown into prison. In the middle of the night, they were chained in the darkest deepest part of the jail. They were numb with unthinkable pain. And they were praying out loud and singing songs of praise to God.

Paul and Silas' joy in persecution became a witness to the other prisoners and eventually to the jailer. Before the morning came, Paul and Silas were free, and the prison warden and his family were new followers of Jesus. There is something unique about a joyful person who is able to stand strong even when beaten down. Doors open for the gospel when a believer follows the biblical exhortation to "rejoice in the Lord always" (Phil. 4:4). As is true in most cases, biblical behavior opens the door for a spiritual conversation and the sharing of the good news of Jesus. Paul and Silas added words to their witness and called the jailer and his family to "believe in the Lord Jesus." And when they did, their lives and eternal futures were transformed.

We stand out when we exhibit peace in a world of turmoil. We live in a time of perpetual conflict and polarization, and in many situations, it is difficult to find peace. When disciples of Jesus walk through hard times with a sense of calm and confidence, it turns heads. We have this otherworldly peace because as we read the Scriptures, we are consistently reminded of who we are. We are assured of our salvation. We are told of God's love for us and his grace in us, his mercy toward us, and his fondness for his daughters and sons. Our peace is not based on circumstances or decisions going our way, or the assurance that we will never suffer. Instead, it is rooted in the bold certainty of whose we are and where we are going. Heaven is our home and nothing can take that away. When people ask us why we can be so peace filled in the midst of turmoil, we talk about the Savior, who has called us his own and has prepared a place for us in heaven.

We invite curiosity when heavenly wisdom guides our daily choices. As we feast on the truth of Scripture, we find answers to life's questions and wisdom to help us navigate the turbulent situations we face each day. The unchanging and enduring teaching of the Bible is like an anchor in a storm. People who have no moral moorings feel like they are set adrift in a relativistic world. But Christians have truth to follow and heavenly wisdom to guide us.

Over the years, we've had many nonbelieving friends, neighbors, and family members come to us looking for insight and wisdom in dealing with a tough parenting situation. Rather than give our own advice, again and again we have directed them to the teaching of the Bible. Because we love, know, and follow the Bible, we have been able to share it with nonbelieving parents, and they, too, have seen the wisdom of God guide them. This inevitably leads to deeper conversations about the Bible, faith, and Jesus.

If we love the Word of God, we will learn to love each person he allows us to encounter. If we know the Scriptures, we will hear the call to go and make disciples of all nations. If we follow the teaching of the Bible, we will walk in the steps of Jesus, which lead us to the broken, hurting, forgotten, and lost sheep he longs to save. Bible engagement leads us out into the world with the heart and message of Jesus.

PART 2

Passionate Prayer

How Talking with God Opens Our Hearts to the World

Jesus was in constant communication with his Father and prayed for his followers and for those who were still wandering far from fellowship with God. As disciples, praying should be like breathing. We can live in intimate communication with the God who made us and loves us. As we grow in the spiritual marker of passionate prayer, we will find ourselves praying for and with those who still need to discover and embrace the amazing grace of Jesus.

CHAPTER 7

Talking to the Father

As Kevin and I write this book, we have been married for thirty-seven years and have known each other for thirty-nine. Through all of those years, prayer has been a significant part of our relationship. Both of us prayed for our future spouses before we met each other. Prior to our first date in the summer of 1982, we had already prayed together, even as we were becoming friends. When we were dating long-distance and living in different time zones, we set a time each day when we knew we would be praying at the same time. It made us feel closer even though we were two thousand miles apart. Once we were married, we decided that praying as a couple would be a priority for us. After almost two decades, three sons, and years of partnership in ministry, we had a good cadence of making time to sit down and pray as a couple a few times each week.

Then something changed. Our prayer rhythm shifted. Instead of setting a time to sit together and pray about specific topics, we started praying throughout the day. When a need arose, we talked with God, even if we were driving or taking a walk. If we were surprised by joy, we thanked Jesus and celebrated his goodness at that very moment, whether we were with each other or thousands of miles apart. When we were talking about one of our boys, a ministry challenge, or a decision, we moved naturally into prayer and then back into conversation. Since that shift in our prayer life, we have moved from praying as a couple a few times a week to dozens of times.

Now we rarely say, "Let's pray." Instead, one of us just begins praying and the other joins in. Sometimes we don't give an official "amen," because we have a sense we are not done praying. Both of us now talk with God this way with a growing number of our Christian friends and partners in ministry. We are discovering that the apostle Paul's invitation to "pray continually" (1 Thess. 5:17) is about feeling free to talk with our heavenly Father during the flow of everyday life.

We learned this prayer practice by watching Jesus. All through the Gospels, we find the Savior in communion with his Father. Jesus prayed constantly. Sometimes in a crowd, at other times with a small group, and regularly in times of solitude. Our Lord prayed with his closest followers and in front of people who were spiritually curious. Prayer was part of Jesus' lifestyle, and it should be for us as well.

Jesus Prayed during the Flow of Daily Life

As you read the four gospel accounts, you find Jesus praying throughout his day. Our Savior talked with the Father in small bursts of a few sentences (Matt. 11:25–26) and in extensive and long prayers (John 17). He prayed for meals and miracles (Matt. 14:19). Jesus cried out to the Father as he healed people (Mark 7:34), and he adopted Scripture as his prayer while suffering on the cross (Matt. 27:46). The Lord of glory prayed for himself (Mark 14:32–36), for his followers (John 17:6–19), and for you and me (John 17:20–26). Prayer poured out of Jesus in any and every situation.

I (Sherry) started noticing that Jesus often prayed with his eyes wide open. When healing the ears of a deaf man, the Savior "looked up to heaven" (Mark 7:34). When he was feeding the five thousand

and gave thanks to the Father, he was "looking up to heaven" (Luke 9:16). As Jesus lifted up the longest recorded prayer in the Gospels, he "looked toward heaven" (John 17:1). When prayer is lifted up in every situation, we will often have our eyes open like our Savior.

A few years ago, I wrote a book titled *Praying with Eyes Wide Open*.[12] One of the themes of the book is that praying continually means keeping our eyes open some of the time we talk with God. If we pray only when our eyes are closed, we will severely limit the times and places we can talk with our Creator. While I was in the process of writing that book, a dear friend of our family, Nabeel Qureshi, was in our home, and we had a wonderful conversation about some of the themes in the book. I told him, "As far as I can tell, there is no passage in the entire Bible that calls us to close our eyes when we pray. I can't find a single example in the Bible that says people closed their eyes while they were praying."

At the time, Nabeel (who has since gone to be with Jesus after a battle with stomach cancer) was doing a doctoral program in New Testament at Oxford. He told me he wasn't sure I was correct on this idea, but that he would do some research. Sometime later, Nabeel checked in with me to let me know that after his research, he could not find a single passage in the Bible that instructs us to close our eyes when we pray. In addition, he could not find any examples of people closing their eyes when they prayed.

This does not mean that closing our eyes in prayer is wrong. I love to close my eyes during certain times of prayer because it helps me focus. The exhortation to pray continually means that all postures are appropriate if we are going to live into this call.

The Priority of Prayer

There is a popular quote often attributed to the great reformer Martin Luther: "I have so much to do that I shall spend the first three hours in prayer." The idea of setting aside time for focused prayer should not stand in contrast to times of speaking with our Lord with our eyes open (and closed) during the flow of a day. In addition to Jesus' constant conversation with the Father, he also made a priority of setting time aside for intense communion in prayer.

At the beginning of Mark's Gospel, we get a glimpse into a day in the life of our Savior. On the Sabbath day, Jesus went to the synagogue to preach. In the midst of the service, he set a man free from demonic attack (Mark 1:21–28). From the synagogue, Jesus went to the home of Simon and Andrew. Instead of being allowed to rest, the Lord ended up leading a time of healing for Peter's mother-in-law (Mark 1:29–31). That same evening, when the Sabbath was complete and people could move around again, crowds flocked to the home where Jesus and the disciples were staying. A revival meeting broke out, and Jesus healed many and delivered others from demons until late into the night (Mark 1:32–34).

After all that, we might expect Jesus to post a Do Not Disturb sign and get some well-earned rest. Instead, early the next morning, before the sun was up, the Savior got up and took a walk to a quiet and solitary place with one thing in mind. He needed, wanted, and was compelled to talk with his Father in prayer (Mark 1:35–37). Jesus made it a practice to find significant chunks of time to get face to face with the Father and commune with him.

As Jesus healed people, set people free, and taught the good news, the crowds grew and demands on him multiplied. Yet even while his popularity was growing and his notoriety was expanding, Jesus still made time for quiet and prayer. In the Gospel of Luke, right after Jesus healed a man with leprosy, we learn that word about the Lord was spreading and the crowds were growing (Luke 5:12–15). But Luke writes that in the midst of all this activity, "Jesus often withdrew to lonely places and prayed" (v. 16). Later in the same gospel, we read about Jesus' conversation with his disciples concerning who he really was (Luke 9:18–20). As Luke sets the scene, he writes, "Once when Jesus was praying in private . . ." (v. 18). These subtle indicators make it crystal clear that Jesus not only prayed in the regular rhythm of life, he also prioritized times for focused conversation alone with his Father.

Prayer in the Big Moments

Arriving at a crossroads, making important decisions, experiencing times of deep joy, facing heart-numbing sorrow—these moments are ripe opportunities for prayer. A survey of Jesus' three years of public ministry reveals that our Savior sought the face of the Father and cried out to him in the major decisions and turning points of his life.

Calling his apostles (Luke 6:12–16). As Jesus expanded his ministry, he called twelve men to be with him and share in the work. As a prelude to this decision, Jesus went up on a mountainside and spent the night praying to God.

The transfiguration (Luke 9:28–36). Jesus took three of his closest friends up on a mountain, and there his glory was revealed. Jesus' appearance shone with heavenly glory, like lightning. Moses and Elijah showed up and talked with the Lord, and God the Father spoke, and they all heard his affirmation of Jesus. This was a big deal! Have you ever noticed how this experience started? Jesus took these three men up on the mountain to pray (v. 28). Everything else that happened grew out of that time of prayer.

The resurrection of Lazarus (John 11:38–44). Jesus spoke in a loud voice, "Lazarus, come out!" and a man who had been dead for four days stood up and walked out of a grave. Amazing! Once again, it is good to rewind and see what our Savior did preceding this staggering miracle. John records our Lord's words: "Father, I thank you that you have heard me. I knew that you always hear me, but I said this for the benefit of the people standing here, that they may believe that you sent me" (vv. 41–42). Jesus prayed out loud so everyone could hear and give glory to the Father.

The garden of Gethsemane, preparing for the cross (Matt. 26:36–46; Mark 14:32–42; Luke 22:39–46). One of the most breathtaking examples of prayer in Jesus' life comes right before he went to the cross. Three of the gospel writers record this time of prayer when Jesus went to the garden of Gethsemane with some of his closest friends and ministry partners. He passionately prayed to his Father over and over again. His prayer was for the cup of suffering to be taken from him, but only if this was the will of the Father. During this time of agony, sorrow, trouble, and spiritual battle, Jesus' sweat became like drops of blood and fell to the ground (Luke 22:44). Not only did he pray in this time of intense struggle, he also called upon the disciples to pray so that they would not fall into temptation. It was in this time of prayer that Jesus firmly resolved to drink the cup and go to the cross.

On the cross (Luke 23:34, 46; Mark 15:34). While Jesus hung on the cross, bearing our sins and experiencing the judgment we deserved, he spoke seven times. Three of these "words from the cross" were directed to his Father—they were prayers. In the physical pain and the spiritual agony of his suffering, Jesus asked his Father to forgive sinful people who did not know what they were doing to him—a prayer of grace. While gasping for air under the suffocating torture of crucifixion, our Lord prayed the opening words of Psalm 22 and asked why he was forsaken—a prayer of loneliness. As he drew to the end of his life, Jesus told his Father that he committed his spirit into his hands—a prayer of surrender. In these final hours of his life on this earth, Jesus continually spoke with his Father.

Being a disciple means seeking to live like our Lord. Praying before, during, and after the big moments of life was normal behavior for Jesus, and it should be for us as well.

Jesus Prayed for His Followers

In John 17, we find the longest recorded prayer of our Savior, often called the High Priestly Prayer. Jesus focused his prayer on the gospel, on his followers, and on those who would one day place their faith in him. Many Christians through the ages have used the Lord's Prayer (Matt. 6:9–13) as a model for how they speak to God. This is a wonderful spiritual discipline, and it would be wise to also add this powerful High Priestly Prayer of Jesus to help shape our conversations with God.

Jesus begins this prayer focusing on the truth and good news of the salvation found in him alone. Jesus cries out, "Father, the hour has come. Glorify your Son, that your Son may glorify you" (John 17:1). The good news of the gospel brings glory to God every time someone proclaims it, hears it, or receives it. Jesus acknowledges he has authority to give eternal life and that this life comes through knowing him. Our Savior goes on to declare that his work on earth will be complete. Before he returns to the presence of the Father, he will finish his mission. A short time later, on the cross, Jesus will declare, "It is finished" (John 19:30).

Next, our Lord prays for his disciples (John 17:6–19). This prayer overflows to all followers of Jesus in all places at all times, and we know our Lord still intercedes for us today (Rom. 8:34). Take note of five things Jesus prays for his followers and let these prayers encourage, inspire, and challenge you.

1. *Jesus prays for protection from the evil one.* Though we are sent into the world and live in a difficult environment, our Savior prays for the very name of our God to protect us.
2. *Our Lord asks for us to experience unity as the people of God.* Jesus goes so far as to pray that we would be one with other believers, just as Jesus is one with the Father. That is a staggering picture of unity.
3. *The Savior asks for his followers to know a depth of joy beyond their imagination.* Jesus wants you and me to experience the full measure of his joy within us.
4. *Jesus prays for us to be sanctified by the truth of his Word.* In a

world of confusion, compromise, and deception, our Savior
prays for us to be saturated with the truth of his Word.

5. *Finally, the great Evangelist and Shepherd of the sheep prays
for us as he sends us into the world.* He compares our being
sent to how the Father sent his Son into the world. That is
a high calling!

Look back at the things Jesus prayed—and still prays—for you
as his disciple. Jesus prayed this when he walked the earth two
thousand years ago, and he is still interceding for these things for
us today.

Finally, we see how the Lord of the harvest turns his heart and
prayers to all those who would come to faith in the years, decades,
and centuries ahead (John 17:20–26). Jesus prays for those who
would hear the good news of the gospel through the disciples in
that generation and in every generation to follow. This is what Jesus
prayed for you before you ever placed your faith in him. It is what
he prays for your friends, neighbors, and family members who still
have not received his amazing grace.

- May they find *unity*, oneness, and true family love. Jesus
  knows that every lost person is disconnected and needs to
  belong. He prays they will find their place of true peace and
  meaning in the family of God.
- May they discover *intimacy* with their Creator. Our Lord
  knows that every soul longs to be united with God and
  restored to relationship with him. Jesus prays for this to
  become a reality for every wandering sheep.
- May they become a *witness* to the world. Jesus delights in
  generational faith and discipleship. Right here in this amazing prayer, we hear the Lord of glory praying for his disciples.
  He also lifts up those who would come to faith through their
  witness. Finally, he prays that these new followers would help

the world see who Jesus is so they can embrace him as well. Jesus paints a picture of hands locked as generation after generation comes to faith.

Every follower of Jesus can learn from this prayer. We should delight that Jesus, the Lord of glory, would pray this for us and every lost person. We can use this as a guide as we pray for loved ones who do not yet know Jesus. You might want to pause, right now, and think of a person you care about who has not yet received the amazing grace of Jesus. Then join Jesus in praying for them to meet, love, and follow the Savior.

CHAPTER 8

Does God Really Want to Hear from Me?

On December 9, 2006, the band U2 performed at Aloha Stadium. It was the final show in the Vertigo world tour, a tour that had spanned two years. More than 45,000 people attended this sold-out event, and we happened to be two of them! A close friend had invited us to join a group of ministry leaders for a few days in Hawaii, and he covered the cost. We rode their coattails to experience this amazing, once-in-a-lifetime concert under the Hawaiian sky.

When we finally returned to the hotel after an hour in postconcert traffic, we were ready to call it a night. As we were about to doze off, I (Kevin) realized I had left my wallet in the rental car and had left the windows down. I hurried to the parking lot and quickly grabbed my wallet. As I was walking back to the hotel, I bumped into two of the women who were part of our group. They were looking at a map, and I asked what they were up to. They said they had an invitation to attend the afterparty with U2 and Pearl Jam on the USS *Missouri* and were trying to figure out how to get there.

It was well after midnight. I knew the route to Pearl Harbor, so I offered to drive them and sleep in the car while they went to the party. They were grateful for the offer and took me up on it, and they even invited Sherry and me to join them. It turned out they had four passes, but their husbands were too tired. Once again we joyfully rode the coattails of someone else, going where we could not have gone on our own.

When we arrived, the party was winding down. The members of both bands were friendly and low key. We had a chance to meet the members of Pearl Jam and even had a nice visit with U2's lead guitar player, the Edge, and his wife. Everyone was hanging out on the deck of the ship (which also happens to be the site where the Empire of Japan surrendered at the end of World War II). The only person missing, that we could see, was Bono, the lead singer of U2.

We learned that he had a private space and people were brought to him for a set time to visit. A meeting with Bono required an additional invitation and an escort to his location. The two women who had invited us also had invitations to meet with Bono, but we were not on that list. They enjoyed a great visit with him and apologized profusely that we could not join them. We assured them we were indescribably honored that we had been able to attend the concert *and* the afterparty. We had no complaints.

As Sherry and I talked about this experience, it led us to an interesting comparison of that night in Hawaii to the ancient temple in Jerusalem. We had both attended Christian colleges and seminaries and had studied the architecture and use of the temple. We recognized some similarities between our night at the U2 concert and the temple courtyard.

In Jesus' day, the temple had a series of barriers and stopping points. Everyone was invited into the courtyard of the gentiles. As Jesus reminded people in his day, this space in the temple was intended to be a place of prayer for the nations (Matt. 21:12–13). Jewish women were invited to come closer to the holy place, beyond the courtyard, but there was a point where they, too, had to stop. Jewish men could come even closer to the temple, but there was a point where they could go no farther and only priests were invited. In the temple itself, a curtain partitioned off the most holy place, and only the high priest could enter that space, and then only once a year (Heb. 9:7). In this place rested the ark of the covenant, where the ancient Jewish people believed the presence of God resided. The curtain was a dividing point, a symbol of the separation between a sinful people and a perfectly holy God.

When Jesus died on the cross, at the moment he gave up his spirit, the curtain in the temple that kept people out of the holy of holies was torn in two from top to bottom (Matt. 27:51). This was a divine invitation, a physical sign that the way to God Almighty was now open and there was no more division. God welcomes us to himself, and every human being has access to God's presence through faith in Jesus.

There are plenty of invitations Sherry and I have not received in our lives. We have never been to the White House. The queen has not invited us to Buckingham Palace for tea. Or, if she has, our invitation got lost in the mail. That night in Hawaii, we knew that Bono's handlers had not given approval for us to meet with him. We rode the coattails of friends and acquaintances to Hawaii, the concert, and even the afterparty. But there was still a divider between us and Bono. And honestly, we were fine with that.

But the God of the universe sent his only Son to enter human history and give his life for all of us. He tore the curtain in two, with divine hands, from top to bottom. The way to God is now open. He is our Abba, our Father, and through faith in Jesus, we are always welcome. The most holy place is accessible, and the most holy God welcomes us with open arms. Sherry and I will take that over a ten-minute time slot with a rock star anytime.

If you ever wonder whether God wants to hear from you or spend time with you, remember what he did to open the way and bring you to himself. Every time you pray, you declare with confidence that God's arms are open and you are welcome in his presence.

When Does God Want to Hear from Us?

God never intended our faith to be relegated to a one-day-a-week experience. He certainly does not want us to limit our relationship with him to a single hour during a formal worship service. Biblical faith is about connecting with our Maker all day, every day. When the apostle Paul wrote, "Pray continually," he was not saying we have to talk with God every second of every day. The good news is that we can talk with him at any time. God is always available. His door is open, his heart is ready, and we know this because the curtain has been torn in two.

In the early pages of the Bible, parents were encouraged to teach faith to their children at home and while walking down the road. This was a reminder that a relationship with God should be experienced at all times and in all places. To help us engage in communion with our Maker, we are encouraged to put reminders around our homes to trigger conversations about God and to remind us to pray to him (Deut. 6:4–9).

The Bible is filled with stories of people praying in times of victory, in moments of defeat, and even in the midst of battle. The Psalms are a collection of prayers for every situation and season of life. Why do you think God devoted the longest book of the Bible (Psalms) to the topic of prayer? Why would God give us so many examples of prayers that can be lifted up in the sweetest moments of joy and in the deepest times of sorrow? The message is clear. God wants to hear from us. Prayer is for right now. Every moment is the perfect time to talk with God. If you paused your reading at this moment and cried out to God, you can be 100 percent certain that his ear is turned toward and tuned to you.

One of the best ways to launch into a good day is to make prayer the first thing you do. About twenty years ago, I (Sherry) started praying first thing in the morning. The way it began was both humorous and amazing. As I was drifting off to sleep one night, I was listening to a sermon. I was fading in and out, so I was only catching bits and pieces of the message. I remember hearing the pastor ask, "Can you imagine what God might do if everyone listening to this message would wake up tomorrow morning, get on their knees, and begin their day in prayer?" A short time later, I dozed off.

The next morning, when I woke, I found myself on my knees next to my bed. I had no conscious thought or memory of getting out of bed. Yet when I opened my eyes, I was already on my knees. A vague memory of what I'd heard in the sermon the night before flooded my mind, and I remember thinking, "This is pretty cool." I took some time to pray there beside my bed and then got up with a fresh new perspective as I moved into the day.

I fell asleep that night exhausted and not thinking about what had happened that morning. To my amazement, when I woke up the next day, I was on my knees again. It was both mysterious and thrilling. It felt like a mini miracle. Again, I prayed and moved into my day with fresh excitement.

The third morning when I woke up, I expected to find myself on my knees. Instead, as I opened my eyes, I realized I was lying flat on my back, under my covers, in bed. I remember one word going through my mind: "Bummer!" I had hoped to have another day when I woke up on my knees.

At that moment, I heard God speak to me. I don't hear God with my ears, but I do receive strong impressions in my heart and even sense words that I am confident are whispers of the Holy Spirit. What I heard in my heart were these three words: "Now you choose." I was confident this was from the Lord, so I rolled out of bed onto my knees and started my day in prayer: "Yes, Lord, I will choose to start my day on my knees, talking to you as the first thing I do. And I commit to do this for the rest of my life." This has been a daily practice ever since. The only thing that has changed since that day is a sense that the Lord had called me to read Ephesians

6:10–18 after praying first thing in the morning. This passage is about putting on spiritual armor and standing strong for Jesus. It is God's way of reminding me of the reality of the battle and telling me that with him, I will stand.

As followers of the Savior, we can begin our day talking to God. We can end each day lifting up prayers of thanks, praise, confession, supplication, or whatever is on our hearts. And of course, we can pray all day between waking and going to sleep. The starting point of a life saturated with passionate prayer is knowing that God longs to hear from us all the time, whatever we are experiencing.

What Does God Want to Hear from Us?

If we are going to talk with God in every situation, we need to have a wide variety of ways to pray. Simple memorized scripts won't get the job done. "Now I lay me down to sleep, I pray the Lord my soul to keep" will get old very quickly. We need to learn how to be honest and tell God everything that is on our hearts. This is one of the reasons the book of Psalms is so loved. It covers every emotion and situation we can imagine, and maybe some we can't.

When we are feeling *thankful* and profoundly aware of the good things God has done and his generous provision or protection, prayers should burst from our hearts and lips. Psalms contains many examples of individual and community prayers of thanksgiving (18, 30, 34, 40, 66, 92, 116, 138, among others). We can make prayers of thanks a reflexive response in the rhythm of every day. To cultivate an attitude of thankfulness, you may want to consider writing down a gratitude list to God at the beginning or end of your day.

We all have moments when we recognize that our hearts, minds, or actions have wandered off the path. Although we are saved by grace and cleansed by the sacrifice of Jesus, we still sin and need to make time for *confession*. This kind of prayer is cleansing for the soul and honoring to God. Psalm 51 was lifted up by David after he had taken another man's wife and then put her husband in a position where his life would be snuffed out. David's prayer of confession can guide us to discover the depth and sincerity of cries to God that come from a truly repentant heart. Confession is so important that James calls believers to have courage to confess their sins to each other and then pray for one another (James 5:16).

When the glory of God breaks into our lives and we get a glimpse of our holy, loving, powerful, gracious Savior, prayers of *praise* erupt. God delights when his children celebrate who he is, his character and attributes. Many psalms focus on praise (95, 96, 98, 100, 147–50, along with others). If we keep our hearts attentive to God's presence and goodness, we will find that prayers of celebration come naturally and frequently.

When loss crashes down, sorrow moves in and won't leave, and discouragement or depression lingers in our souls, God invites us to lift up prayers of *lament*. These are honest prayers expressing our hurt, fear, sadness, and struggle. Most prayers of lament also acknowledge that God is on the throne and can be trusted, even though the situation is painful and feels unbearable. What is shocking is that of all the prayers in the book of Psalms, lament is the most common. More than one-third of the psalms are laments (3, 4, 12, 13, 22, 31, 39, 42–44, 57, 61, 71, 77, 80, 94, and many more). Too often Christians think they need to bury their hurt and deny their pain. God invites us to come to him with unfiltered honesty and pour out our hearts to him.[13] Laments almost always end with an expression of trust that God is sovereign and on the throne.

All of us have moments when we desperately need direction. We face situations that we simply can't navigate. In the book of James, God calls us to pray to him with bold confidence when we lack wisdom (James 1:5). Prayers for *wisdom* are also modeled in the book of Psalms (37, 49, 73, 112, 127, 128, 133, and others). God wants us to come to him for guidance and direction as we make complex decisions and also the little choices of life.

The book of Psalms also offers prayers for times when injustice and evil are at hand. These are called *imprecatory* prayers (35, 69, 83, 88, 109, 137, 140, 143, among others). We can feel a bit uncomfortable reading these raw and sharp-edged cries to God. Some of these prayers include expressions like "strike my enemies," "bring shame on them," and "break their teeth." A call for justice is often embedded in imprecatory prayers. One beautiful thing about these shocking cries to God is that they teach us to come to him in the toughest of times and hold nothing back. They show us that there are times our anger is best brought to the throne of God and not the doorstep of the person who has hurt us.

Why would God give us a book in the Bible that offers examples of prayers for every situation and season? He wants to hear from us no matter what the day brings. God knows we will have times of ecstasy and moments of sorrow. Both are perfect times to talk with him. We will have victories and deep losses. Prayer should accompany these times. No matter what we face, prayer can be our continual practice.

Prayer Lessons from Jesus

The life of a disciple is about continual growth as we become more like Jesus. He modeled the marker of passionate prayer. Not only did he live as an example of constant and intimate communion with the Father, he also taught us about prayer. You can read the four gospels and do your own study of Jesus' prayer lessons, but here are some things we've learned about prayer from our study of Jesus' life.

The power of prayer (Mark 11:22–25). Prayer can cast mountains into the sea, free people from demonic control, heal bodies, restore broken relationships, unleash heavenly power, and so much more. The only limit to God-honoring prayer is the power of God, and he is omnipotent. Jesus wants us to know there is more power in prayer than we dream. As we pray, we should do so with absolute faith that

God can do all things. This does not mean we can demand what God will do. We ask in faith and God determines what prayers will receive a heavenly yes.

Only by prayer (Mark 9:14–29). There are times when our abilities, efforts, and sincerest longings will not accomplish what God desires in this world. Some things will be accomplished only through prayer and the heavenly power it unleashes. Jesus' disciples learned this when they tried to minister to a boy who was possessed by an evil spirit. Apparently, they had tried everything they could think of—except prayer. When Jesus came on the scene and cast out the demon, the disciples asked why they could not get the job done. Jesus was emphatic: "This kind can come out only by prayer" (v. 29). When we come to the point when nothing we try seems to get the job done, why not pray? Or better yet, why not begin with prayer?

Crazy prayer (Luke 6:27–31). Jesus made some declarations that must have sounded downright crazy when they came out of his mouth. "Love your enemies." "Do good to those who hate you." "If someone slaps you on one cheek, turn to them the other also." Right in the middle of this run of seemingly absurd declarations, Jesus said, "Pray for those who mistreat you." In the context of this passage, it does not sound like Jesus was calling them to lift up an imprecatory prayer (prayer for God's judgment). Rather, he wanted them to pray a prayer of blessing and grace. One of the prayer lessons Jesus wants to teach us is that we should pray for people who mean us harm or who have already hurt us. Rather than a knee-jerk response of retaliation, reflexive prayers of grace should pour from our hearts and lips.

Shameless and audacious prayer (Luke 11:1–13). In the first thirteen verses of Luke 11, we find some of the most amazing teaching on prayer offered by our Savior. It begins with Jesus praying and the disciples asking him to teach them to pray. Next, we find Luke's record of the Lord's Prayer. (The version found in Matthew 6 is more commonly known.) After this, Jesus tells a story about prayer. The bottom line is obvious: when we pray, we should ask with "shameless audacity," as the friend does in the story. Keep knocking. Keep asking. Be bold. It is clear that the story Jesus is telling us is about prayer because everything before and after this story is focused on prayer. God loves his children. He wants to give good gifts. Our part is to ask with bold confidence.

Persistent prayer (Luke 18:1–8). Later in Luke's Gospel, Jesus taught another lesson through a story about prayer. This time it was a widow coming to a judge seeking justice. She was relentless. It was clear she would never stop. So the judge gave in. He answered her request. Jesus is teaching us never to give up as we pray. The point of the story is not to say that God answers because he grows weary of our whining and relentless requests. God is nothing like the judge in the story. Our God is a loving Father and he longs to bless his children, so we should never stop asking. Our prayers are not a bother to our loving Father.

We learned this lesson over forty-four years of prayer. My (Kevin's) father raised his five children as agnostics/atheists. One by one, each of us became followers of Jesus, and three of us ended up doing some kind of Christian service. We all prayed for our dad faithfully and persistently, over months, years, and decades. There were many times it seemed he would never open his heart to the love, grace, and friendship of Jesus. We did not stop praying. Others joined us. Sherry made prayer for my dad as much a part of her life as it was mine. Thousands of faithful Christians joined in. I believe there may have been tens of thousands of people all over the world faithfully praying for my dad's salvation, because everywhere Sherry and I spoke for the last three decades, we asked people to pray for my dad, Terry.

Forty-four years after I became a Christian, my dad received Jesus as his friend, leader, and forgiver of his sins. Sherry and I had the honor of being with him when he surrendered his heart to the

Savior at eighty-four years old. My dad went to be with Jesus just a month after receiving this gift of grace. We are deeply thankful for the persistent prayers of so many.

Surrendered prayer (Matt. 26:36–46). When Jesus was drawing near the end of his life, he lifted up an example of prayer that should influence every one of his followers. "Not as I will, but as you will." Whatever we pray should be wrapped in the language of and in an attitude of utter surrender. We are flawed and can pray selfishly or wrongly. Only God is omniscient and has the wisdom to rule the universe. When we surrender to his will, we are growing as disciples.

Springboard prayers (Matt. 6:9–13). When the disciples asked Jesus to teach them to pray, it was clear that he was not giving them a memorized prayer to be regurgitated over and over like a mindless mantra. Unfortunately, some people have turned the Lord's Prayer into the very thing Jesus spoke against. The Lord's Prayer is meant to be a springboard into the deep waters of conversation with our heavenly Father. Each line carries a wealth of meaning that can move us to thousands of different prayers.

When we pray, "Give us today our daily bread," it is a springboard for more specific prayers for ourselves and the people we love. "Lord, our daughter is struggling at her job and she is on the edge financially. Please provide the right job and economic stability so they can make ends meet." Or, "Our church is struggling to meet our ministry budget, but we believe you want us to minister to our church members and the lost in our community. Please help your people grow in generosity to provide what your church needs." You get the picture. Jesus gave example prayers not to be memorized and repeated but to launch us into heartfelt petitions.

Just a quick note to those who are in a church tradition that lifts up the Lord's Prayer every week in worship. There is nothing wrong with committing a prayer to memory and reciting it in community. But be sure to let the themes of the prayer move you to deep communication with God beyond the mere recitation of the words.

Evangelistic prayer (Matt. 9:35–38). Jesus taught his followers to pray for a great harvest of souls. This was a longing of our Savior's heart and should be a defining part of our prayer lives. What is interesting is that Jesus also calls us to pray for ourselves. With compassion in his heart and awareness of the needs of lost sheep, our Savior said, "Ask the Lord of the harvest, therefore, to send out workers into his harvest field" (v. 38). Jesus understood that a significant problem in the evangelistic equation is that many of his disciples are not going out into the fields. We need to pray for ourselves. "God, in your power, move me, use me. Here I am, send me!"[14]

Divine alignment in prayer. No matter what kind of prayer we lift up, a faithful follower of the Savior will always do one thing consistently: we will pray in the name of Jesus. Our Lord said, "And I will do whatever you ask in my name, so that the Father may be glorified in the Son. You may ask me for anything in my name, and I will do it" (John 14:13–14).

What does it mean to pray in the name of Jesus? It does not mean that you will get whatever you want if you tag the words "in the name of Jesus" on the end of your prayer. Using Jesus' name is not a way to sanctify every prayer so that God is obligated to say yes.

In the ancient world, a person's name was a reflection of their character. To speak in someone's name was to represent them at a core level. To do something in the name of another person was to align with their will, wishes, desires. When we pray in the name of Jesus, we are saying, "This is a prayer that honors Jesus. It comes from his heart, it aligns with his will, so I pray it in his glorious name."

Praying in the name of Jesus is the opposite of what some people think. It is not making a list of our desires and whims and using the authority of Jesus' name to get what we want. It is finding divine alignment in prayer by lifting up those things that honor

Jesus and sync up with his wise will. When we do this, we are praying in his name, even if we don't finish our prayer with the words, "In the name of Jesus."

Prayer Warnings

Not only does our Lord teach us how to pray, he loves us enough to give some sobering warnings about how not to pray and what prayer is not about.

No performance prayers (Matt. 6:5–6). Jesus made it clear that prayer is about communing with God, not impressing people. Some religious folks in his day knew how to lift up extraordinary prayers in just the right place, with perfect words, in front of just the right people. When they were done, everyone was mesmerized—except God. Their Creator knew they were not talking to him but performing before other people. Jesus made it crystal clear that we are to make sure our prayers are to God, for God, and not to impress the people who might be listening.

Beware of mindless repetition (Matt. 6:7–8). The key to growing deeper in prayer is not to memorize and parrot the same prayer over and over. In Jesus' day, there were people who did this. They had set prayers for certain times, places, and situations. Just dial up the right prayer for the correct setting and recite it. But these recitations had no heart, no mental engagement, and not even a sense of really speaking to God. It was about heaping up the right words and saying them over and over. And Jesus made it clear: don't babble and pile up empty words and pretend this is prayer. Don't recite mindless phrases and think you are talking with God. Instead, engage in meaningful communication with the God who loves to hear from you.

No prideful prayers (Luke 18:9–14). Jesus loved stories and understood their power to teach and to rivet truth to our souls. In a heartfelt teaching moment, Jesus told a story about two men who went to pray. One was a religious leader, and he stood before the Lord and lifted up a prayer celebrating how wonderful, devoted, and generous he was. The other was a tax collector who was profoundly aware of his own sin and brokenness. He approached God with deep humility and a meek spirit. Jesus made it clear: God gladly received the prayers of the second man.

4 Generation Challenge (2-2-2)

How do we lock hands in prayer with those who are influencing us in our spiritual development? How do we partner with the people we are seeking to help grow in the marker of passionate prayer?

Make prayer like conversation. I (Kevin) have the honor of investing in the spiritual growth of our church board members. In particular, there are two men on our leadership team who have served as "enduring members." This means they are exempt from the rule of serving no more than two terms in a row. Both of them were on the board when I came and have continued to serve for many years.

I began spending time with each of them, and we prayed together regularly. Sometimes it was in a social setting, while at other times we were doing church work. Whatever the setting, prayer seemed to flow naturally into our time together. Over the years, it became so natural that I found myself praying with them much like Sherry and I pray together. I would not say, "Let's pray." We would simply be talking and I would move right into praying. In the course of our time together, we could often end up praying three or four times.

About a decade into our friendship and relationship, both of these men began doing the same thing. We never talked about it. It just happened. Both started moving into prayer with me in the flow of our time together. Often there is no particular moment when someone says, "Let's pray," or a specific need is shared. We just pray. Sometimes we say amen, and at other times we just move back to the conversation. It is beautiful.

Make mealtime prayers a daily practice. It can seem like a lost practice, but there is something intimate and honoring to God about prayer around a table. I (Sherry) grew up in a home where we had dinner as a family every evening. My mother and father led us in prayer before every meal. We learned to recognize that food on the table was a gift from God. I and my siblings might have wiggled and squirmed a bit, but we could feel the sacredness of this moment as we saw grown-ups talk with God like a friend. We learned that things happened in our lives, family, and the world because people prayed. We witnessed it every day.

Kevin and I carried this practice into our family life. We placed a high value on meals around the table and always prayed together as a family. We would invite our three sons to lift up short sentence prayers of thanks. We would often pray for the two children our family sponsored. Their pictures were on our refrigerator, and we were familiar with their faces and needs. As parents, Kevin and I took the hands of our children and taught them what I had learned from my parents.

As we were in the midst of writing this portion of the book, we went to Michigan to visit our youngest son, Nate, and his wife, Brynne, and their two beautiful children, Coen and Piper. Piper is just saying her first words, but Coen is quite verbal and loves to pray. Sometimes after I pray with him, he will say, "More prayer, Maga!" (Maga was Coen's early attempt at saying Grandma, but he switched the order of the syllables. It made us laugh every time, so he decided he liked it and it stuck.) During our visit, we shared a meal with them, and Nate led in the family prayer. He asked each of us to lift up a thank-you prayer. When it was Coen's turn to pray, he said, "Thank you for pot stickers." It was a joy for us to hear, and we believe God was delighted with this simple and heartfelt prayer.

Let's trace this beautiful generational prayer pathway. Sherwin and Joan Vliem taught me and my siblings the value of family prayer at the table. Kevin and I taught this to our three sons, Zach, Josh, and Nate. Nate and Brynne are now teaching Coen and Piper, and Coen is joining in family prayer. You can do the math, but I count four generations. Hands and hearts locked together growing in faith. Oh, the beauty of discipleship!

Praying Out Loud

It would likely surprise most people who know me well, but I (Sherry) was afraid to pray out loud when I went away to college. I became a resident assistant (RA) in one of the dorms at Calvin University in Grand Rapids, Michigan, and I was excited to encourage the young women on my floor, support them, and be a friend to them. That first week, I found out I was expected to lead in prayer at our dorm meetings. The thought of doing this made me sick to my stomach. I loved Jesus, read my Bible faithfully, and was excited about my faith, but I was not comfortable praying out loud.

I shared this fear with my roommate Connie, a godly young woman who was also assigned to be an RA on our floor, and she did something amazing. She discipled me. Connie said, "Sherry, you and I are going to pray together, out loud, every morning. We will keep doing it until you feel comfortable."

She took my hand and led me forward in passionate prayer, and through that experience I matured. When we had our first floor meeting, I led everyone in prayer. This was a tremendous gift from a dear Christian friend.

Over the past twenty years, I have had the honor of teaching many people to grow more peace filled and confident in prayer, including learning how to pray out loud. I have had the humbling privilege of writing a book on prayer and speaking to many people about this topic. I would not be where I am today in my prayer life if it were not for people like my college roommate, who took my hand and helped me climb upward on my journey of faith.

What is your next step in deepening your commitment to passionate prayer? Who is holding your hand and helping you grow in this wonderful part of your faith journey? Whose hand are you holding as you help them connect more intimately with God? How will the world be different in ten years—and in a hundred years—because you prayed and helped others seek God in prayer with growing passion?

CHAPTER 9

Praying for and with the World

In 2019, just before the covid-19 pandemic hit, we had an amazing opportunity to do a series of evangelism trainings for students, pastors, church leaders, denominational leaders, and seminary professors.[15] The participants were hungry to learn and stayed attentive through ten hours of learning. One of the ideas I (Sherry) taught was how God shows up when we pray with people who are not yet Christians. The idea of talking to God, out loud, with a nonbeliever is new to many followers of Jesus. Invariably, when people get this concept, it excites them and moves them into a whole new world of prayer and evangelism.

As Christians, we believe in prayer. We might even dare to tell a nonbelieving friend, "I'll be praying for you." But entering a time of prayer with a non-Christian can feel off limits. The truth is that both Kevin and I frequently ask nonbelievers to pray with us and almost all of them say yes. Over the years, this has included hundreds and hundreds of people ranging from hardcore atheists to curious agnostics to friendly people who just don't think much about spiritual things. Not only do these people welcome prayer, but it clearly means a great deal to them. They often shed tears when we pray for them. It is a grace-filled moment.

I taught this concept at an Organic Outreach Intensive Training and challenged all the participants to ask the Lord each morning to help them see open doors to pray with people who are still far from God. One of the women took this challenge seriously and found an opportunity the next day as she headed home from the training. She sent me an email and gave me permission to share it with others:

Hi Kevin and Sherry,

I just attended the training in Melbourne. I want to share that I prayed the prayer you encouraged us to pray, Sherry, this morning when I woke up for the second day of the training. As we were leaving the conference to walk to the train station, we were looking to get a coffee on the way. We paused at one place, but my husband decided to look further. A few meters farther on, we passed a young lady sitting on the steps of a building, crying and looking at her phone. We briefly locked eyes and she quickly looked down.

We walked a few more paces and then I said to my husband, "That girl is crying." He asked me whether I wanted to go and talk to her and God gave me the courage to do that. I still had the last talk you gave at the conference going through my mind, so I asked her if she was alright, could I do anything, or would she like to talk to me, to which she replied, "No, no, I'll be okay." I felt prompted to ask again: "Are you sure?"

Then she told me that she was having a panic attack and she was supposed to be at work and her boss would be wondering where she was and now she had to ring and try to explain. So I took it straight from the conference and told her that I was a Christian and that God had helped me through times like this and would she like me to pray for her, to which she said, "Yes, that would be nice." I deliberately kept my eyes open and prayed for God's peace and comfort to come to her and that she would be able to make the phone call and also get to work.

She watched me through the whole prayer, and when I finished, a beautiful smile came over her face. She said, "Thank you, that was very helpful." I gave her a gentle hug and said, "Just remember that I prayed to Jesus, and if you are in need, you can call to him and he will meet you." I left her smiling on the steps, feeling that my task was finished. Later I started to wonder whether God had put her there for me more than me for her.

Praying *with* Spiritually Hungry People

This sweet woman, sitting on the stairs in the middle of a panic attack, is just one of the countless people who need a touch of God's presence and grace. How many people do we walk past because we don't see their need? Every time a Christian prays with a nonbeliever, God shows up. We could fill the rest of this book with stories of amazing things God has done in these sacred prayer moments. Rather than tell our stories, we want to help you create opportunities of your own.

The first step in growing a practice of unleashing God's presence through praying with spiritually hungry people is to believe that many of them will welcome prayer and say yes when we ask. The only way to grow this conviction is to start offering prayer and see what happens. Over time, you will learn that most people are open to prayer. If they are not, the worst pushback most of us will face is having someone say, "No, thanks! That's not my thing." Few of us will face true persecution just for offering prayer.

The second step is keeping our eyes and hearts open. Consider starting your day asking the Spirit to help you slow down and notice moments when you can offer prayer.

We can ask the Holy Spirit to show us when a person sitting alone on the steps might need prayer, a gracious word, and a touch from Jesus. We may not be able to tell, but God is ready to guide us.

The third step is having courage to ask. "Thanks for telling me about the birth of your granddaughter. I would be honored to say a little prayer for her and for you, if that's okay." "I am so sorry to hear your father has learned he has cancer. I would love to pray for your dad if you would feel comfortable with that. We don't need to close our eyes. God is here with us and he hears the cry of your heart. Is that okay with you?" You might want to develop a practice of offering prayer for your server when you dine in a restaurant. "Hey, when our food arrives, we are going to say a quick prayer. If you have a need or joy you would be willing to share with us, we would be delighted to pray for you. No pressure, just let us know if you think of anything." Many servers will share a need right away. Some of the prayer requests will be shockingly personal. Some servers get busy and don't circle back to the topic. If that happens, don't push it. Your part is to make the offer and follow through if they share a need or joy.

The fourth step is to pray. Don't use religious language, don't preach a sermon, be brief, ask God to move in their life in the specific area they shared, and pray in the name of Jesus. It is amazing how God shows up and moves in these sweet moments.

The fifth and final step is to follow up. If you prayed for a health issue, the next time you see that person, ask how it is going. If you lifted up thanks for the birth of a grandchild and asked for God to bring joy to a new grandma or grandpa, ask how the little one is doing. Keep their prayer need in your heart and follow up when appropriate.

We have lots of friends who have learned to do this same kind of prayer outreach right where they live. Walt Bennett, the CEO of Organic Outreach International, and his wife, Liz, had a dynamic experience praying with a spiritually hungry person. She was the roughest and gruffest checker at a store they frequented. Walt and Liz were determined to get to know her better, so they would get in her line every time they saw her, even if it was the longest one. Over weeks and months, through one or two thoughtful questions at a time, they learned about her family and her favorite activities. They knew when she was heading out on vacation and when she was having a good or bad day. One day, they noticed that she looked particularly dour. They asked her what was going on, and she shared that she had just received a text informing her that her sister had received a cancer diagnosis. They immediately asked if it would be alright if they prayed for her. With a look of disbelief, she gave the okay. It was just a quick prayer for healing for her sister, wisdom for the doctors, peace and strength for her. The people behind them looked on, not in frustration but in respectful silence and some fascination. When they finished praying, they could see the tears in the cashier's eyes and the huge relief reflected in her posture and countenance. In the coming months, they checked in on how her sister was doing and received improving reports to the point when her sister was cancer free. What a simple but powerful example of paying attention and praying for a spiritually hungry person!

A Praying Christian Sends Powerful Messages

When we have an active and authentic prayer life and nonbelievers know it, they learn by watching and listening to us. There are all sorts of messages that spiritually curious people will see and hear when we are open about what prayer means in our lives.

God is real or I am unstable. If we talk to God regularly and believe he hears us, there are only two options. There is a God who listens and loves us, or we are talking to a make-believe being in the sky (and that would be a sign of mental instability). When a Christian prays consistently and knows God hears, it sends a powerful message: God is real. In truth, God is the most real person I know.

I have an intimate friend. In a world where so many people feel abandoned, lonely, and hungry for a true friend, Christians know the greatest friend a person could ever have. Jesus himself called his followers friends (John 15:15), and when we walk with our Lord, talk to our heavenly Father, and follow the leading of the Holy Spirit, we commune with the one who is real and really with us. He is Immanuel, God with us. We are never alone. A passionate prayer life shows the world that we have a friend in Jesus and he is ready to be their friend too.

God answers prayer. Every follower of Jesus has stories of answered prayer. We can share these, at the right time and in the right way, with our nonbelieving friends and family members. When we do this, they will often ask questions. "Do you really think God did that?" "So you believe God protected you in that situation?" "You truly think God had a part in your finding that new job?" When people ask these questions, most of them are not wondering about our faith or sanity. They are curious about whether there is a God who could come near them, hear their needs, and answer their prayers. In those moments, we can assure them that God loves them and has power to answer their prayers.

God is powerful. In a world where many feel powerless and caught by the whims of bosses, world movements, uncertain stock markets, and so many other things that seem out of control, it is stabilizing to know that God is on the throne. The one to whom we pray has all power, and we can live in that peace. When we come to God in prayer, share our fears and burdens, and walk in peace, the world notices. People who speak often with God live in confident peace because they know who rules the universe. Non-Christians notice our confidence in God's power and it becomes a witness.

Prayer Aligns Our Hearts with God's Heart for the World

Our God cares about those who are lost and wandering. When Jesus saw the crowds of people, he felt deep compassion. He knew they were just like sheep, vulnerable, wandering, in danger of attack

(Matt. 9:36). All through the Bible, we learn that God loves us. Even when people rebel and run away, God cares and pursues them.

It is easy for Christians to get frustrated or angry with non-believers. Instead of seeing people through the gracious eyes of Jesus, we can become judgmental and bitter because of how they live, talk, and behave. It is possible for followers of Jesus to be upset with non-Christians because they don't act like Christians. Just think about how silly this is. Why would we expect those who are not in love with Jesus or filled with the Holy Spirit to have the desire or power to live in godly ways? It is hard enough for Christians to live like Christians, and we walk in the power of the Holy Spirit.

When we pray and spend time in the presence of our gracious God, our hearts are shaped by his heart. Our wills conform to his. Our thinking aligns with the God who loves lost sheep. How do prayer and evangelism connect? The more time we spend communing with our God in prayer, the more we will look like him, think his thoughts, and love as he loves.

Prayer Changes and Softens Hearts

For almost a decade, we prayed for Henry. He was a hog farmer, a joke teller, a family man, and an atheist. Kevin built a friendship with him, and he was a delight to be with, as long as you did not bring up Jesus or any spiritual stuff. I (Sherry) was close friends with his daughter, Deb, so we prayed that his heart would soften. I decided that I wanted to grow in a regular practice of praying for his salvation. I realized that I drove past his house about a dozen times in the course of a normal week, so I decided to use driving past his house as a reminder to pray for him. I took this commitment seriously, and for almost a decade, thousands of prayers were lifted up for Henry as I drove past his house.

When Henry ended up in the hospital with cancer, we all prayed even harder. Through the prayers of God's people and the tender work of the Holy Spirit, Henry cried out to receive the grace of Jesus, and he entered a relationship with God near the end of his life. He had a vision of Jesus, which he described to his daughter, and surrendered to the Savior.

To an outside observer, it could have looked like this conversion came overnight. We know it was the work of God through constant, faithful, passionate prayers that prepared and softened Henry's heart for that very moment. As you pray for people who seem resistant, don't give up. When you have been praying and a person seems to be growing even harder toward the gospel, don't stop. Something happens every time you pray. There will be times that we don't notice the softening power the Spirit unleashes through prayer until the day a person receives Jesus.

An Invitation to the Ultimate Prayer

There will be people in your life whom you pray for countless times. They are far from Jesus, but you love them, so you pray. You ask the Holy Spirit to soften their hearts. You pray for opportunities to talk about faith. Maybe you have prayed with them many times through the years. I (Kevin) prayed with my dad almost every time I was with him for more than twenty years, but he had not said yes to Jesus. I also prayed for his heart to soften almost every day for more than four decades.

But there was always one prayer missing. There comes a moment when we feel the prompting of God's Spirit to ask, "Are you ready to pray and receive Jesus as your forgiver and the leader of your life?" This is the ultimate question that can lead to the ultimate prayer. When you feel the prompting to ask this question, a spiritual battle will rage. The enemy will unleash distractions, fears, and lies. This is when we stand strong and cry to God, "Give me courage and guide my words."

When Sherry and I were with my dad in the last month of his

life, we had a great visit. We laughed, talked, shared memories about my mom, and prayed. We had engaged in countless spiritual conversations, discussions, and debates over forty-four years. At one moment on that trip, I followed the Holy Spirit's nudge to ask him, "Dad, can you think of any reason you would not receive Jesus as your leader and forgiver right now?" He thought for a moment and said, "Not that I can think of!" I paused and then said, "Are you ready to pray and confess your sins and accept Jesus?" He said, with bold conviction, "Absolutely!"

After forty-four years of walking this road, I was shocked. I should have been ready for this, but he had pushed back so many times that I was braced for another rejection. I paused and asked him again, "Dad, are you sure you are ready to pray and confess your sins and accept Jesus?" He said it again: "Absolutely!" For the next few minutes, Sherry and I had the joy of praying with my dad as he confessed his sin, declared faith in Jesus, and articulated his desire to take Jesus' hand and follow him the rest of his life and for eternity. I was so grateful for the opportunity to offer the gift of salvation and have him accept Jesus as his personal Lord and Savior. It was the last time I saw him.

When you come to that moment with a friend, neighbor, stranger, or family member, be ready to lead them in the ultimate prayer. We have a couple of simple resources on our website to help you prepare for that moment.[16]

Passionate Prayer Draws People to Jesus and Moves Us into the World

If you want to go deeper into the topic of sharing your faith naturally, we have written three books to help you: one for individuals, one for families, and one for churches.[17] In addition to what we share in those books, here are some quick and easy to adopt ideas for how your prayers can impact people with the good news of Jesus.

Make us one. Jesus prayed for his followers to be united as one, even as the divine Son and Father are one. Into our divided and conflicted relationships, our Lord prayed for unity (John 17). If we are going to be part of God's plan to bring peace and harmony, we must learn to pray against the things that drive wedges between people and groups.

Prejudice and racism look for a place to take root in every heart. We can pray against these evils in us and in others. We can confess where our attitudes, motives, or actions have been tainted by these sins. As we pray, we can do our part to seek unity and fellowship with people who are different from us. Jesus came to make us one, and he prayed for this with relentless passion. So should we.

1-1-1 prayer. We were privileged to have author Lee Strobel come to speak at the Organic Outreach conference we held at our church in Monterey. As Lee taught on prayer and evangelism, he encouraged people to adopt the practice of doing what he called a 1-1-1 prayer. The idea is simple and powerful. Each day at 1:00 p.m. you pray for one minute for one person who is not yet a Christ follower.

Many of our church staff set an alarm on their phones for 1:00 p.m. with the name of someone they loved. It was a sweet reminder of prayers being lifted up when at 1:00 p.m. we heard phone alarms going off. After doing this for some months, I (Sherry) realized that 1:00 p.m. was really not a good time for me to have my phone alarm ring. I decided that the evening afforded a more focused time for me to pray. I changed my alarm to 9:00 p.m., and when it rang, Kevin and I paused to pray for his dad. Instead of doing a 1-1-1 prayer, I adopted what I refer to as my 9-1-1 call.

Kevin's dad was the person I had been praying for every night at 9:00 p.m. After Terry received Jesus, when the alarm went off at 9:00 p.m. that next night, we paused to thank God that Terry had received Jesus, and we prayed for his growth as a new follower of Jesus. Now when my phone alarm sounds at 9:00 p.m., I pray for a new person and I thank God for the power of prayer, trusting my new 9-1-1 call will have eternal impact. After this prayer, I often pause and think of my father-in-law, Terry, and the joy he must be experiencing with Jesus in glory.

Psalms and other Bible passages as prayers. As you talk with people who are going through times of stress, loss, or fear, consider giving them a psalm (or some other biblical prayer) to lift up as their own prayer. People who do not have faith are often open to prayer during the hard times. Psalm 23 is fairly familiar, but most nonbelievers have never considered making it their own prayer. As spiritually hungry nonbelievers begin praying, God draws near.

When someone is in a time of great gratitude and thankfulness, offer a Bible passage that expresses praise and gratefulness to God. Let them know that praying this passage can unleash their heart to the God who provides all they have and who loves them. It is hard to feel thankful and not know who to express it to. By giving a nonbeliever a psalm of praise or a prayer of thanksgiving from the Bible, we connect them to their Creator and to the Scriptures at the same time.

Listening prayers: Good God questions. God can connect prayer and outreach when we learn to listen for the leading and prompting of the Holy Spirit. This kind of listening can be guided by what we call "good God questions." These are questions we can ask God and wait quietly for the Spirit to whisper to us and guide us. Here are some examples:

- Who would you have me serve in your name to reflect the care of Jesus?
- How much do you love this person, and will you teach me to love as you do?
- What story of faith or testimony of your work in my life should I share with my non-Christian friend?
- Spirit of God, will you open my eyes to see opportunities to care for nonbelieving people, love them, and pray for and with them?

Open doors and divine appointments. God is looking for followers of his Son who will walk through open doors and accept divine gospel appointments. There are people who are open and hungry to learn more about Jesus and to meet the one who loves them. Our part is not to create these moments but to respond when God leads.

Every day, we can ask God to give us opportunities to love people in his name. Then we can respond and let the adventure begin. I (Sherry) was standing in line at the Los Angeles airport waiting for an international flight. I serve on the board of World Mission and was joining a team to do some ministry and training of church leaders. We were in line for quite some time when I sensed the Holy Spirit nudge me to turn around and engage with the woman behind me. I had no idea where this would lead, but I have learned that every time I respond to the Holy Spirit's whisper, I am being faithful. I asked the woman if her trip was for business or pleasure. I think the word *pleasure* caught her off guard. She replied that it wasn't for business, but it was not going to be pleasurable. She said that she was flying to deal with some family problems that had to be addressed. She was careful not to share details but was open with how difficult the situation was. I sympathized with her.

I let her know that I believed God cared about what she was about to enter and that I would love to ask for God's help for her. I shared that God was with us even as we were standing in line and that we could call on him. I let her know we didn't need to close our eyes but just have a conversation with God and ask for his help. After we prayed, we talked more and exchanged contact information.

A few months later, I received a very sweet email from her thanking me for the few moments of friendship she felt I had given to her at that stressful time. She let me know that things were even worse than she had thought but wanted me to know she felt that the prayers really did help and that she had experienced comfort and strength during that difficult trip. She ended her email by sharing that she felt it was no coincidence she had met me.

If you feel a nudging of the Holy Spirit to offer prayer during a conversation, be faithful to God's leading and trust that God is at work through you as you interact with those around you who need a touch of his Spirit.

Passionate prayer and evangelism are bound together in the heart of God. As we recognize this and engage more in prayer, God will move us outward with the good news, love, and truth of Jesus.[18]

PART 3

Wholehearted Worship

*How Praise, Celebration, and Worship Propel
Us Outward and Draw the World In*

Wholehearted
Worship

Our God is worthy of worship! Disciples find delight in giving praise, glory, and honor to the only one who deserves it. When we grow in faith, worship flows from our hearts and lips. Every experience of life can be a place for worshiping in Spirit and in truth. When the world sees Christians who celebrate the goodness of God, overflow with joy, and walk in humble surrender, they become curious. When groups of believers gather and celebrate with overflowing joy and passion, the world wants to know more and we can tell them our story.

CHAPTER 10

Worthy of Worship

In my senior year of college, I (Kevin) served as a youth pastor at a church in Southern California. I had volunteered with youth groups since I became a follower of Jesus five years earlier and absolutely loved helping students grow in faith. But this was different. This church actually hired me, put me on staff, and let me lead a group of young people. It was humbling and exciting at the same time.

There was a high school student named Ted who came from a tough background. He had faced abuse, neglect, and some pretty intense stuff in his life. Yet by God's grace, he had put his faith in Jesus. He was passionate about following the Savior, but it is fair to say he was still pretty early in the sanctification process and had some rough edges. When he got mad about something, you could see the rage and hurt rising to the surface. This tough, strong, passionate young Christian was trying his best to grow as a follower of Jesus.

In one of our group gatherings, we were talking about worship. I asked the students, "How would you define or describe worship?" A number of them gave nice, brief, church-kid answers. They were helpful, but they certainly did not breathe passion. Then Ted spoke up with intensity and absolute seriousness. His words left a hush over the room and have never left my heart (and that was almost four decades ago).

"I don't bow to anyone. If someone tries to push me down or knock me over, I'll fight back and keep standing. But every single day, I get on my knees and bow down before Jesus. He is God! He is *my* God! That's what I think worship is."

Surrender. To prostrate oneself in willful obedience, bowing down. This is a powerful picture of worship.

Jesus Was Worshiped

From the very beginning of his time on earth, people worshiped Jesus. Wise men from the east came with the express intention of honoring him (Matt. 2:1–2). When they finally found the baby, they did three things: they bowed down, worshiped, and gave gifts. Before Jesus had done anything (except being born), the wisest of people came to worship him.

Many years later, near the end of his time of ministry, our Lord entered Jerusalem and the crowds shouted:

> "Hosanna!"
> "Blessed is he who comes in the name of the Lord!"
> "Blessed is the coming kingdom of our father David!"
> "Hosanna in the highest heaven!"
>
> —Mark 11:9–10

Spontaneous cries of worship were lifted up to Jesus.

When our Lord relinquished his life and died on the cross, a soldier declared, "Surely this man was the Son of God!" (Mark 15:39). We are told that after Jesus ascended to heaven, his followers "worshiped him" (Luke 24:52). All through his time on earth, people bowed down and praised Jesus.

In each of these settings, Jesus had no control over what these people said or did. When the wise men came, Jesus was just a baby. When he entered Jerusalem before his death, the crowds cried out before him. When the soldier worshiped him, Jesus had just died. And when the disciples worshiped him, Jesus had just ascended to heaven.

Maybe all of these people were wrong. Perhaps Jesus would have corrected them if he'd had a chance to say something. Could it be they were overly zealous and wrong in expressing their worship of Jesus? Some have claimed that all these people were wrong to bow down and worship.

What would Jesus say?

Jesus Freely Received Worship

All we need to do to answer that question is to watch how Jesus responded to the passionate acts of worship people extended to him. How did he react when he was lavished with the praise only God deserves?

- When Nathanael came to meet Jesus as a skeptic and cautious critic, he quickly changed his tune and declared, "You are the Son of God; you are the king of Israel" (John 1:49). If Jesus was only a rabbi, he would have shut down that way of speaking immediately. Instead, Jesus said, "Very truly I tell you, you will see 'heaven open, and the angels of God ascending and descending on' the Son of Man" (John 1:51). Now that's taking it up a notch!
- All three of the Synoptic Gospels (Matthew, Mark, and Luke) record the account of Jesus' going up onto the mountain with Peter, James, and John. While there, many things happened, but one powerful moment is when Yahweh spoke and said, "This is my Son, whom I love. Listen to him!"

(Mark 9:7). In the presence of the disciples, the Father exalted Jesus, the glorious Son. Jesus gave no rebuttal and made no complaint.

- After Jesus walked on the water and Peter joined him, Jesus climbed into the boat and we read, "Those who were in the boat worshiped him, saying, 'Truly you are the Son of God'" (Matt. 14:33). Everyone who witnessed the power and glory of Jesus was moved to spontaneous worship. It is clear that Jesus, the Son of God, was perfectly comfortable with this.

- The entire ninth chapter of John's Gospel is devoted to the story of a man born blind whom Jesus healed. Near the end of the account, Jesus has a pastoral conversation with the healed man and our Savior revealed himself as the Son of Man. The man's response was brief but powerful. The Scriptures reveal what he said and what he did: "'Lord, I believe,' and he worshiped him" (John 9:38). Not only did Jesus freely accept this man's worship, but he explained that he had power to judge and heal both physically and spiritually. Are you getting the picture? Jesus affirmed people who worshiped him.

- In an encounter in the temple courtyard area, Jesus drove out the vendors and affirmed that God's house is a place of prayer. The religious leaders chastised Jesus and the children because the little ones were crying out, "Hosanna to the Son of David" (Matt. 21:15). They were lifting up praise to Jesus. Instead of agreeing with the chief priests and rebuking the children, Jesus quoted from Psalm 8: "From the lips of children and infants you, Lord, have called forth your praise" (Matt. 21:16). Jesus cheered on those who were worshiping him and declared that they were perfectly in line with Scripture.

- The stories of Jesus being anointed with valuable perfume are found in all four of the gospels, displaying wholehearted worship (Matt. 26:6–13; Mark 14:3–9; Luke 7:36–50; John

12:1–8). In each case, people were upset by this "waste." In every account, it is clear that Jesus freely received these acts of surrender, sacrifice, and celebration.

- After Jesus died on the cross and bore our sins, he appeared to his followers in resurrection glory. Again and again, people worshiped him. Each time, Jesus gladly received their words and acts of adoration. When Jesus encountered Mary Magdalene and the other Mary as they hurried away from the empty tomb, they bowed down, took his feet, and worshiped the risen Lord (Matt. 28:1–10). Jesus encouraged their actions and instructed them to tell the disciples they would see him soon. When Thomas expressed his doubt that Jesus had risen and finally saw him face to face, he cried out, "My Lord and my God!" (John 20:28). Jesus did not rebuke him but declared that people will be even more blessed if they come to the same conclusion as Thomas without having to see Jesus raised from the grave. Finally, when the disciples met Jesus right before his ascension to heaven, they worshiped him (Matt. 28:17).

When worship was directed toward Jesus, he received it every time.

Jesus Inspired People to Worship the Father

Not only did Jesus welcome and delight in the worship people showed him, but his life, words, and actions moved people to worship the Father. Over and over, we see people responding with praise as Jesus revealed the presence, power, and glory of God.

Right before he fed the four thousand, Jesus took time to heal people who were sick, broken, and hurting. The crowds were amazed. Interestingly, their response was not to praise Jesus directly. "They praised the God of Israel" (Matt. 15:31). Our Lord's actions moved people to praise God. When they praised the God of Israel, they were also praising Jesus.

When a group of friends brought a paralyzed man to Jesus and "airlifted" him through a hole in someone's roof, Jesus used this moment to heal, forgive, and teach (Luke 5:17–26). By the end of the story, two things happened. First, the man who had entered the room paralyzed got up and walked out under his own power, praising God with each step. Second, everyone who had gathered in that house was amazed and lifted up praise to God. It is clear Jesus believed in worship, because his life propelled people upward with praise to his Father.

After Jesus healed ten men of leprosy, one came back to thank him and praise the Father (Luke 17:11–19). This man's act of worship and commitment to return and express his heart to Jesus and the Father led our Savior to celebrate his faith.

When a blind beggar screamed over the noise of a crowd, "Jesus, Son of David, have mercy on me!" (Luke 18:38), the Lord took notice. Jesus had a conversation with him and spoke words of healing. When the man received his sight, he followed the Lord and began giving public praise to God. In response, people in the crowd also began giving praise to God. Jesus inspired multiplying praise.

Not only did people worship Jesus, and not only did he gladly receive praise reserved for God, but Jesus inspired others to worship and celebrate the goodness of the Father.

Jesus Taught His Followers to Worship

By example and through formal teaching, our Savior instructed his followers how to worship and engage with our heavenly Father. Most of the lessons came in the flow of Jesus' interacting with real people in real time. If we listen to the Savior's conversations about faith and worship, we will gain valuable insights for how we, too, can grow as worshipers.

Beware of merging worship and commercialism. When Jesus walked into the courtyard of the temple, he did not find a place conducive to encountering the Father (Mark 11:15–17). He did not see a place of prayer, worship, and adoration. It was more like a swap meet or a flea market. Vendors were selling their products for worship. Animals were everywhere, waiting to be purchased and offered in ritual sacrifice or given as offerings. It was chaotic!

The courtyard where this was happening was the one area on the temple grounds where the nations (the non-Jewish people) were invited to come and meet with the God of Israel, often referred to as Yahweh. Now it had become a center of trade and commercialism. The sales being conducted were connected with the temple worship, so it could have seemed justifiable. But Jesus did not view it that way. When the marketing, sales, and promotion of religious products become the driving goal of our "worship," we have crossed a line. This was the case in Jesus' day, and it is just as true today.

Some people won't get it! Of all the people in the ancient religious establishment, the high priest should have recognized the Messiah and worshiped him. Even the elders and teachers had immersed themselves in the Scriptures for a lifetime. They knew the prophecies and promises of a coming Savior. As this group of leaders put Jesus on trial, they asked him, "Are you the Messiah, the Son of the Blessed One?" Jesus responded, "I am" (Mark 14:61–62). "I am" was the divine name Yahweh used for himself when Moses stood before the burning bush in the wilderness (Ex. 3:14). Jesus then doubled down and declared that they would see him sitting at the right hand of Yahweh and coming on the clouds of heaven.

This was the moment for them to see with eyes of faith. God in human flesh stood right in front of them. The Messiah had come. The appropriate response would have been to bow down, worship, and submit to his leadership. Instead, they spit in his face. They punched the one who had left heaven to save them, and they mocked their Messiah.

Jesus made it crystal clear who he was. But not everyone got it. And even today, not all who hear of God's love and offer of forgiveness will bow their knee to Jesus. Some will refuse to worship. In every generation, some will mock God and slander him and spit in his face. Yet none of these things change who Jesus is or the worship he deserves.

You're gonna worship someone or something. After Jesus had spent forty days fasting in the wilderness, the devil came to tempt him (Luke 4:1–13). In his second assault, the enemy offered the Lord authority and the splendor of the kingdoms of the world if he would do one thing. Worship Satan. Bow down and surrender to his evil will.

Jesus' response was simple and clear. He quoted from the book of Deuteronomy: "Worship the Lord your God and serve him only" (Luke 4:8). Why did Jesus quote these words and lift up this truth written in Deuteronomy 6:13? Because we will all face the temptation to bow down, pledge our allegiance, and surrender our hearts and devotion to something or someone other than God. Jesus was clear about who he was, and he taught that all who walk in his ways will worship only God.

It's not the where but the heart. Jesus had a robust and dynamic theological conversation with a sinful Samaritan woman while sitting at a well near her hometown (John 4:4–30). Not only did this break the rules for rabbinical behavior in the first century, but it led to Jesus' teaching about worship. In that part of the world, at that time, there was a huge debate over where people should worship. Was Mount Zion the proper place? That's what the Jews believed. Was Mount Gerizim the best place to meet God? The Samaritans held this view. Jesus said something radical and revolutionary. "A time is coming when you will worship the Father neither on this mountain nor in Jerusalem" (John 4:21). For a Jewish rabbi to speak this way was akin to blasphemy. But Jesus said it and meant it. The location is not the issue.

What really matters is that we "worship the Father in the Spirit and in truth" (John 4:23). The heartbeat of worship is people who are led by the Spirit of the living God. This can happen anywhere. Our priority is to worship in the truth of God more than in a set location. Jesus made it clear that the Father is searching for people who encounter him with hearts filled with the Spirit and minds immersed in the truth. This delights our Creator.

If we want to grow as wholehearted worshipers, the best thing we can do is watch Jesus, listen to his words, and follow his leadership. This is what it means to be a disciple.

Living in obedience to the will of the Father is an act of surrender. Worship is about surrender. More than songs and emotions, it is about bowing down, both physically and spiritually. Jesus surrendered to the will of his Father over and over again.

The apostle Paul puts it this way: "Therefore, I urge you, brothers and sisters, in view of God's mercy, to offer your bodies as a living sacrifice, holy and pleasing to God—this is your true and proper worship. Do not conform to the pattern of this world, but be transformed by the renewing of your mind. Then you will be able to test and approve what God's will is—his good, pleasing and perfect will" (Rom. 12:1–2). Jesus lived a life of sacrifice, surrender, and alignment with the will of his Father, and that is the pattern for his followers as well.

Honoring and glorifying God is worship. Whenever we seek to bring glory to God, to lift up his name and honor him, we are engaging in worship. Jesus teaches us to do this. As he drew near the end of his life and prepared to go to the cross, Jesus cried out, "Father, glorify your name!" (John 12:28). At the Last Supper, after Judas left to betray him, Jesus spoke these words: "Now the Son of Man is glorified and God is glorified in him. If God is glorified in him, God will glorify the Son in himself, and will glorify him at once" (John 13:31–32). What a powerful picture of the Godhead in mutual celebration! In his High Priestly Prayer, the first thing

Jesus said as he looked upward to heaven and began praying was, "Father, the hour has come. Glorify your Son, that your Son may glorify you" (John 17:1).

Jesus surrendered his life, his words, and his praise to the Father. As we follow Jesus and grow as disciples, we will worship with growing passion. This will lead us into the world to invite the nations to meet the one who is worthy of all praise, honor, and glory.

CHAPTER 11

Worship as a Lifestyle

- A church building filled with passionate Christians singing songs of praise.
- A teenager on the beach looking at the crashing waves, blue sky, and countless grains of sand and whispering, "Wow, God, nice job!"
- A business leader seeking to prayerfully make God-honoring decisions day after day in the complexity of a secular work environment.
- A couple walking hand in hand and taking turns lifting up prayers of thanks and praise.
- An artist sculpting, painting, singing, dancing, or playing their instrument with absolute focus on bringing glory to God.
- A group of friends sitting together and watching a sunset as they discuss ways to follow Jesus in different areas of their lives and offering all they are as living sacrifices to their good Creator.

Which of these is worship?

The answer should be obvious after studying the life of Jesus. True worship is about a life surrendered to the Father, who made us and loves us. What is our true and proper worship? "To offer your bodies [all we are] as a living sacrifice, holy and pleasing to God" (Rom. 12:1).

Worship can and should erupt continually, wherever we are, whatever we are doing.

Worship All Week Long

I (Kevin) was working at 7-Eleven shortly after I became a follower of Jesus. Some of my best worship times that summer, after my sophomore year of high school, were in a giant freezer as I was stocking six-packs of Pepsi and Budweiser. I would spend a couple of hours each shift in the massive cooler breaking down boxes, stacking cases of drinks, and refilling all the holders so thirsty people could find their beverages. The fans and coolers made it hard to hear, so I sang as loudly as I could. I did not know any hymns or church songs, but I was learning some nice praise choruses at youth group, so I sang those. When I ran out of songs, I just made them up. Words of adoration came to my heart, and I shouted, sang, and celebrated God's goodness while working. Every so often, someone would open one of the clear glass doors to grab a single or a six-pack. There would be a suction and then the sound in the cooler would change. Sometimes I stopped singing, but at other times, I just kept praising God. The customers might have thought a madman was locked in the freezer, but the worship in my heart kept flowing, so I kept going.

I daresay that one of the most beautiful cathedrals I have ever worshiped in was that big drink cooler at the 7-Eleven. I met Jesus there. The wind of the Holy Spirit was even greater than the fans of the freezer. My heavenly Father and the creator of the universe showed up and met with a sixteen-year-old kid who was just figuring out what it means to be a worshiper. "Jesus replied, 'Believe me, a time is coming when you will worship the Father neither on this mountain nor in Jerusalem. . . . Yet a time is coming and has now come when the true worshipers will worship the Father in the Spirit and in truth, for they are the kind of worshipers the Father seeks'" (John 4:21–23).

Worship is surrender and obedience to God. Jesus lived in continual obedience to the Father. As we learn to walk in the footsteps of our Savior, we will honor God by surrendering to his will and ways. If we show up every Sunday for church but rebel against God's will the rest of the week, how is this a life of worship? When we give God the leftovers and scraps (Mal. 1:6–11) and keep the best for ourselves, we are not learning what it means to offer our lives as living sacrifices. We can sing hymns and praise songs with angelic voices, but if we use these same lips to curse people who are made in the image of God, how are we living as worshipers?

None of us has perfect alignment of how people see us during a formal worship service with who we are the rest of the week. But we should be seeking, with all the power of the Holy Spirit, to be consistent in every circumstance. Jesus knew the will of the Father and lived in it moment by moment. As his disciples, this should be our deepest desire: to know the Father's will and obey it. This is our act of worship.

Worship of the Father, Son, and Holy Spirit. There is a beautiful trinitarian aspect to worship. We live to praise the one God: Father, Son, and Holy Spirit. Each person of the Trinity is worthy of worship. In their unity of being, worship is fully appropriate. For many centuries, the Christian church has embraced three ecumenical creeds: the Apostles' Creed, the Nicene Creed, and the Athanasian Creed.[19] In the longest of these creeds, the Athanasian, a significant portion is devoted to the doctrine of the Trinity. Reflect on these words:

> Nothing in this trinity is before or after,
>> nothing is greater or smaller;
>> in their entirety the three persons

are coeternal and coequal with each other.
So in everything, as was said earlier,
we must worship their trinity in their unity
and their unity in their trinity.

An ordinary day can become extraordinary if we listen for the voice and leading of the Holy Spirit and are moved to worship. Every time we notice the beauty of God's creation, we can celebrate his goodness. As we seek to follow Jesus in a way that honors the Father and is led by the Spirit, we will sing, praise, celebrate, stand in awe, bow down, and surrender to the will of the Almighty.

Invite bursts of wonder and awe throughout your day. What propels a follower of Jesus upward in worship? There are many things, but one of the most significant is noticing. When we slow down, open our eyes, pay attention, and take note of God's presence, we will be drawn to deeper worship.

When a cat curls around your leg and turns its tail into a question mark and purrs so loudly you can hear it, pause and give praise to the creator of every furry creature. When you see a dog run and jump for joy, stop and thank God for the simple pleasures of life and let your heart join in the joy. If you see a sky so piercingly blue that your brain has to work hard to register the color, whisper a word of thanks to the God who provides such staggering visual beauty. When you take a bite of a great meal and the flavors explode and bring delight that only culinary treats can deliver, stop and celebrate the God who invented taste buds, flavors, curries, peppers, honey, and fresh fruit.

When God created the heavens and the earth, the apex of his work was people made in his image, complex but beautiful. When you engage with a person who brings joy and meaning to your life, turn your heart upward and thank God. When a child or grandchild falls asleep in your arms, a friend comes to your side in a time of need, a spouse shows tenderness, a neighbor offers help, or any of a thousand other joy-filled interactions takes place, pause to worship the one who made people and declared his creation good.

When you wake up and take a breath of air into your lungs as you begin another day, recognize God's goodness. As you sip a cup of coffee, thank your Creator for making the beans. For the blessing of meaningful work, thank God. When challenges come that strengthen your faith and drive you to your knees in prayer, praise God for his sustaining power. As you find moments to relax, refresh, and play, thank the Great Provider. As you place your head on the pillow at the end of the day, thank God for many things, including the gift of a pillow.

Beware the enticement to worship anything or anyone other than God. If the devil tried to entice Jesus to bow down and worship, why should we think we are exempt from his temptations? Jesus was God in human flesh, and yet the enemy still went after him. Followers of Jesus should expect ongoing attacks and anticipate demonic efforts to shift our allegiance from God to anyone and anything else. Satan does not care what you worship (what you devote yourself to) as long as it is not the one true God.

Though Satan will try any tactic and offer any enticement that he thinks will work, he does have some favorites. As worshipers and followers of Jesus, we need to be vigorous in our efforts to guard our hearts, eyes, schedules, and devotion. Anyone or anything that takes the central place in our lives can become an object of worship. When this happens, God falls to second place, and before we know it, the one we call Lord is in fifteenth place!

Every follower of Jesus should make time, on a regular basis, to examine their heart and life and make sure nothing is taking too high of a place in their affections. What about money and stuff? Jesus gave serious warnings about how material things can become way too important. Ask yourself, "Are there people who mean so much to me that their opinion or approval is more important than God? Does my devotion to a person (spouse, child, grandchild, friend) cause me to compromise my faith or be distracted from fully following Jesus? Do I have a hobby that consumes my time or resources so that I can't serve Jesus, be generous, and live for him? Does my job control my schedule and consume my mind so that I can't live with Jesus as the Lord of every moment of my day? Have I let entertainment and media rule my schedule? Do I spend more time playing video or digital games, watching shows, or surfing the internet than I do sitting at the feet of Jesus? Are my desires and wants driving me so that I am now in charge and setting the direction for my life rather than following the all-wise God, who I declare is my Lord and leader?" If we are going to live as worshipers, it will mean pushing anything and everything else off the throne.

The Power of Gathered Worship

When most of us think of worship, we picture a setting with a group of Christians assembled in a church building. That picture changed for many people in 2020 because of the covid-19 pandemic. In a matter of weeks, people were worshiping in their living rooms, watching on their TVs, tablets, or computers. Some were praising Jesus with earbuds in while watching on their phones. Others began gathering outdoors with social distancing and masks. A lot changed. But much stayed the same.

The rhythm of God's people coming together as a group to worship in community is deeply embedded in the history of the church and in the souls of God's people. There is something uniquely beautiful about the body of Jesus all together worshiping the King of Glory.

It's not all about the place, but the place does matter. Jesus made it clear that the location is not the central issue when it comes to worship (John 4:21). But being in a set place in the community of God's people does matter. Jesus himself, as a twelve-year-old boy, made it clear that his parents should have known where to find him—in the temple of the Lord, talking and learning, in communion with God and in fellowship with others. There is something powerful about regularly meeting with the people of God. In the book of Hebrews, the writer says, "Let us hold unswervingly to the hope we profess, for he who promised is faithful. And let us consider how we may spur one another on toward love and good deeds, not giving up meeting together, as some are in the habit of doing, but encouraging one another—and all the more as you see the Day approaching" (Heb. 10:23–25).

Gathering is important to the heart of God. The Old Testament is filled with feasts and celebrations that drew the people of God together. The ancient Jewish community had a rhythm of weekly worship that was part of the fabric of their lives and faith. Followers of Jesus continue this spiritual practice of gathering to glorify God, encourage each other, celebrate the resurrected Savior, and bear witness to the world. Home churches meet in living rooms. In some parts of the world, small congregations gather under thatched roofs made of palm leaves with no sides. God delights in small country churches that meet in traditional A-frame buildings with a steeple, and the Lord shows up in massive megachurch auditoriums that are equipped with state-of-the-art technology. What matters is not the kind of building but the people who gather in it. Sacred space is made so by the presence of the Holy Spirit at work in the lives of wholehearted worshipers.

Enthusiasm with wisdom. It was Easter Sunday, and we were getting ready for five consecutive worship services. I (Kevin) saw a woman enter our worship center and make her way to the middle of the front row. She was carrying something that looked like two medium-length aluminum pipes. I took note of the unusual objects, but she seemed safe enough. Over the years, I've learned that on occasion, people who come to Shoreline Church will bring strange things with them.

As the service started and the worship team began the first song, the woman unfurled two massive worship flags and started waving them around with great enthusiasm. The people to her left and right had to shimmy away to avoid being whacked. Folks in the row behind her had to duck the poles swinging toward them. One of our pastors approached her and kindly explained that we did not have the space for this kind of activity. She told him she was worshiping and wanted to continue. He gently but firmly clarified our concern that she was going to hurt someone and needed to stop. As the conversation ended, she packed up her flags and left, frustrated that she did not have the freedom to worship with her flags at the front of our worship center.

Enthusiastic worship is encouraged all throughout the Bible. We should come to God with passionate, wholehearted praise and fully engage in giving him the glory he deserves. But when we worship in community, we must be aware of the needs of others and not just fixated on our own experience. To borrow a quote that has been attributed to luminaries such as Oliver Wendell Holmes Jr., John Stuart Mill, and Abraham Lincoln, "My right to swing my fist ends where your nose begins." I am free to act as I like until my actions intrude on your freedom and space. Or to put it in terms the woman at our Easter service could understand, "Your freedom to swing your worship flags ends when you are about to whack a fellow worshiper on the head!"

A humble disciple of Jesus cares about other worshipers. We are free to be expressive and to praise with passion. But if our expression and freedom wrench others out of worship, are we truly following the leading of the Spirit of peace? If my expression shuts down yours, I should care enough to curtail it so we can both give God praise in the same space.

Dealing with distractions. A few years ago, our oldest son was invited to volunteer at another church because they needed a guitar player. When we asked him how it went, he said it was fine, but he was frustrated because the pastor had singled a group of them out during the service.

He explained that after the time of worship in song, he and some others had taken a seat in the worship center and were engaging in the message, reading the Scripture passage with a Bible app on their phone. A few minutes into the sermon, the pastor stopped his message and chastised our son and some of the other young adults for distracting him by playing on their phones during his sermon. He told them to put the devices away and pay attention. The problem was, these young adults were actually following along on their Bible apps. They had not brought any other Bible option. This pastor highlighted two things: first, his ignorance about the widespread use of Bible reading apps today, and second, the very real problem with distractions in worship.

Distractions are a genuine challenge, and technology can be a factor. Many people find Bible reading apps a helpful way for them to engage the Bible in church or away from home. But there are also many times when technology can be a distraction, hindering us from full engagement in worship. If we turn the clock back a few decades, the option of bringing a phone to church simply didn't exist. Today, we have powerful computers we carry around in our pockets and purses, as well as tablets that stream the world into our hands. We have watches that act as conduits for texts, calls, and email, along with information on how many steps we've taken that day, the latest news items and social media updates, and . . . you get the idea. The benefits of staying connected through technology have led to an exponential increase in the potential for distraction.

When we gather to worship, we come into the presence of God Almighty. We join with his people to praise, honor, and adore him. We need to do all we can to limit the distractions and maximize our engagement. If we are easily distracted by our watches, phones, or tablets, we might want to put our devices in airplane mode and carry a printed Bible. Be willing to do whatever it takes to fully engage with God in worship. Ruthlessly remove anything that will get in the way of your encountering the one who deserves your praise.

God-centered worship. Worship is about God, not us. We live in a me-centered world and are led to believe that our enjoyment, edification, and experience are what matter most. This kind of thinking is both juvenile and dangerous. The very concept of worship should direct us away from self-centered thinking, but apparently it does not. Even mature and seasoned believers need to be reminded about this.

Many years ago, I (Sherry) watched a transformation toward spiritual maturity happen through a conversation between my father and my husband. My dad was struggling with some of the new worship music being introduced in his church. Honestly, he liked the older, more familiar hymns, and the new music did not really connect him to God. He expressed this to Kevin, and they had a wonderful conversation. Kevin listened and sought to understand his concerns. But he also asked him a question: "Sherwin, since when did worship become about you?" They talked about how new music could connect with the younger people in the church and help them praise God. They agreed that most of the nonbelievers in the community where my dad lives were not listening to organ music in their cars or homes and that more modern music might connect them to the truth and messages contained in the songs. They talked extensively about the theology and practice of worship, but one refrain came up over and over in that conversation: worship is not about us, it is about God.

Almost immediately, my godly father changed his tune, both metaphorically and literally. I have since heard my dad bring up that conversation several times, sharing how thankful he is for Kevin's boldness to set him straight in that moment. He embraced the new music while still loving the great hymns and songs of the past. He decided to lift his voice to worship God no matter what the style of the music or songs. And he has spread that message to others, initiating the same conversation with other people from his generation who similarly have struggled. My dad has helped others remember who is the center of worship.

4 Generation Challenge (2-2-2)

Again, note the progression in this story about my dad learning to embrace new worship music. My husband, Kevin, who is more than two decades younger than my father, took his hand and helped him gain a new perspective. Kevin spoke truth and my dad realized he needed to grow in maturity as a wholehearted worshiper. My dad discovered that his eyes needed to stay on God and that he could praise the Lord with any style of music. That's maturity!

Next, my dad took the hand of a few of his friends and others in the church who were struggling with the same issue. He talked with them and encouraged them to move beyond their tastes, styles, and likes. My dad challenged some of his contemporaries to get a bit more contemporary when it came to musical styles in worship for the sake of reaching those who do not yet know God's love. I am confident that some of them took the hand of a spouse or friend and helped them grow in the same way. That's four generations of Christians going deeper in worship. That's organic discipleship!

CHAPTER 12

The World Loves a Good Party!

What does worship have to do with evangelism? How can whole-hearted worship draw people closer to the Savior? There are far more connections than most of us recognize. Both our personal lives as worshipers and our gathered worship experiences can give lost people a vision of heaven and create hope for true connection with the divine. The world loves a good party, and worshipers know how to celebrate in the flow of a day, in our homes, workplaces, and social settings, and when gathered with God's people. On top of all this, we live with unbending confidence that we will celebrate with God eternally in heaven. The life of a worshiper should be attractive and compelling and should point people to the God who is worthy of all praise.

Worship as a Lifestyle (Scattered)

As a young girl, I (Sherry) witnessed worship all day, every day. If worship is offering everything we are and do to the God who made us, I can honestly say I watched my parents display the glory and joy of worship continually. Yes, they prayed a lot, read their Bibles, sang hymns, and gave with generous hearts, but it was more than that. My parents walked with Jesus, adored him, and surrendered their wills to the desires of God over and over again. When difficult times came, my mother, with calm confidence, said, "God takes care of his own." My dad led a life of prayer, and when hard times came, talking to God was his first response. As prayers were answered, worship followed. Through the years, my parents have continued to model a lifestyle of worship through all things, even as they said goodbye to their only son, my brother, Mark, when he lost his battle to cancer. Through many tears, they have continued to worship God. For my parents, all of life is worship.

When we worship, even in the hard times, the world looks on in wonder. It is easy to lift praise to God and surrender to his will when things are going our way. In the good times, we should celebrate God's grace and kindness. But the world pays special attention to how Christians behave when the diagnosis is bad, when the economy is in turmoil, and when pain comes crashing down.

We have a dear friend who has been battling Parkinson's disease for more than a decade. Jason lives with the reality that his body is fighting against him every moment of every day. His wife, Leslie, is his partner in life, faith, family, and all they face together. In our more than ten years of friendship with them, we have not heard either of them complain, not even once. They know Jesus. They look to the one who is on the throne of heaven and of their lives. They have surrendered everything to the creator of all things.

Both Jason and Leslie work in the hospitality industry. Through all they have faced, countless people have been inspired by their faith and confidence in God. Because they live with open praise, adoration, and honor of God, their lives shine with Jesus' presence. Of course, there are hard days. Lots of them. They both pray for a cure for this terrible disease. But in the midst of it all, their adoration of the Father is a witness to what a worshiper looks like. Many people have seen the heart of Jesus as they look at Jason, Leslie, and their two adult children. Anyone who knows them can see that they follow the Savior through a storm that shows no sign of ending. Worship like that is a witness to a watching world.

Worshipers emanate the presence of the Holy Spirit. When a Christian lives each day surrendered to God and in a state of worship, the Holy Spirit is present in clear and powerful ways. We have all experienced it. You walk into a home that is saturated with prayer, filled with praise, and occupied by a worshiper, and there is something in the air. People feel it. Nonbelievers might not be able to put it in words, but they can sense something warm, alive, attractive, gracious about it.[20]

The Holy Spirit is present in the lives of worshipers. Believers see it. Spiritually curious people feel it. God is there. This divine presence is a witness to the world. If you are talking with a person who does not know Jesus, and they notice something different in your home, office, cubicle, or life, don't be shy. Tell them that the Spirit of God is near. Commend them for noticing. Then offer to tell them more about this God who dwells with you and lives in you.

We long for deeper worship than this world offers. Christians used to talk and sing about heaven more than we do today. If you go back and study the hymns and songs of old, you will find a strong theme of longing to see God and worship him in glory. When we make worship a central theme in our lives, we will long for much more than this world offers. A hunger to see our Savior face to face will grow.

As the world becomes more conflicted and people are increasingly polarized, there is a yearning for peace, unity, and something lasting and real. We have a message of unending hope and the promise of eternity with the God who made and loves us. As we anticipate the glory that awaits, we can share this hope with a world filled with people who long for more. God's arms are open, and he is ready to wipe their tears away and give them eternal life.

Of all the people in the world, Christians should be the most joyous. Worshipers are filled with gladness. We have seen Jesus. Our sins and the judgment we deserve have been cast into the deepest sea. We have a friend who loves us like no other. In a world where sadness, despair, depression, and discouragement rule, worshipers connect with the God of infinite joy. Through the highs and lows of life, we can still worship and celebrate the God who has already written the last chapter of the book. We know how the story ends. A throne. A crown. Victory! We will be seated with our Savior in heavenly places forever. Our worship has just begun, so our joy is unending.

Christian homes should be saturated with the presence of the living God. We have always sought to make our home a place of grace, fun, celebration, and truth. As we raised our three sons, their friends came over often. Sometimes they even visited us when our sons were not home because they wanted to talk with adults who would listen, care, speak encouragement, present truth, and pray for them. We were always blessed to see how much they trusted us.

One day a friend came over for a visit—a retired NFL player named Rickey Bolden. He exudes joy everywhere he goes. After six seasons on the offensive line of the Cleveland Browns, he retired to become a pastor. The day Rickey dropped by our house, there were about a dozen high school guys hanging out in the basement. They were stunned to meet a six-foot, six-inch tall mountain of a man weighing in at around three hundred pounds.

Rickey circled the guys up and talked about football and what it takes to succeed in professional sports. Then he asked each of the guys how they were doing in school and whether they took their studies seriously. Before you knew it, he was telling them about what it means to be a follower of Jesus in a world that does not always cheer on the Christian faith. He described the surrender, sacrifice, and devotion it took to live for Jesus while playing at the highest level of professional sports.

Some of these young men were not churchgoers or followers of Jesus. They had been in our home over and over through the years and knew that Jesus was the center of all we did. Meeting Rickey and hearing his story of leaving professional football to become a pastor made sense because they had all been in a home devoted to Jesus and had heard these kinds of stories before. When Rickey pulled them in for a huddle and prayer before leaving, they all leaned in and then lined up for a hug from this contagious lover of Jesus.

Worship in Community (Gathered)

If Christians are the most joy-filled people in the world, then the church should be the most joyous community. When we gather to worship our God, the environment should be explosively glorious. If someone walks in who has not met the Savior, they should be drawn to Jesus as they see people deeply in love with him. Most of the people who are far from faith will have their first encounter with God's presence outside a church building as they meet Jesus' people. But something powerful and life-impacting happens when a spiritual seeker walks into a congregation of gathered believers who understand what it means to worship in Spirit and in truth.

True worship is never about us. God is the center of worship, or it is not truly worship. If we act like worship is about me—my style, my tastes, my likes—there is a biblical term for that. Idolatry! If we want guests, friends, family members, and spiritually curious people to encounter God as they visit the church we attend, we need to do all we can to make sure he is on the throne and his glory is on display.

Is worship for those who are still on their way to Jesus? My (Kevin) sister Alison attended a wonderful church in Irvine, California, for a couple of years before she became a follower of Jesus. She made friends. The church welcomed her. She even sang in the choir. It was more than two years of belonging before she believed. When she finally confessed faith in Jesus, I had the honor of baptizing her in the church fountain after a Sunday morning service.

During the baptism, the church choir circled the fountain and sang "Down to the River." I can hear it as I write these words, and it brings tears to my eyes today just as it did many years ago.

> As I went down in the river to pray
> Studying about that good ol' way
> And who shall wear the starry crown
> Good Lord, show me the way
>
> O sisters, let's go down
> Let's go down, come on down
> O sisters, let's go down
> Down in the river to pray

I praise God for Mariners Church and a choir that embraced my sister as they worshiped week by week. I am eternally grateful for a body of believers who love people as they learn and walk toward Jesus. I rejoice that when my sister put faith in the Savior, she was already being discipled and had a community walking with her. This never could have happened if that church believed worship is only for the converted.

Should people be invited to Jesus during worship services? Because many churches invite nonbelievers to join them on their way to discovering Jesus, some Christians find themselves in a strange place. Is the church, and particularly worship services, a place for nonbelievers? In some circles, this is up for debate. We have learned that a congregation can gather, be true to the Scriptures, and have vibrant worship experiences while spiritual seekers are present. As a matter of fact, it is a great place for people who are spiritually hungry. We don't design the service for nonbelievers, but we are fully aware that they are participating.

A worship service is for the glory of God! When the Lord is our consuming passion, believers can join in and give God glory. At the same time, spiritually curious people can watch, learn, feel the presence of the Holy Spirit, hear the truth of Scripture, and decide whether they want to take a next step toward the Savior.

I (Kevin) preach almost every Sunday and have done so for almost three decades. Every time I open God's Word in a church service, I do so knowing there are devoted Christians listening as well as many people who are seeking to discover who God is. In eleven years of pastoring at Shoreline Church, I have made a habit of regularly inviting people to place their faith in Jesus. I do this because I know there are people attending who are not yet Christians.

If I am planning to present the gospel of Jesus and then call for a response, I get our prayer team engaged in preparation two weeks in advance. We also prepare packets for new believers so we can help them move forward as disciples. We have Bibles in English and Spanish ready to hand out. About six to eight times a year, I invite people to publicly respond to the good news and place their faith in Jesus. Because we have three services every Sunday, I have done this more than 230 times over more than a decade at Shoreline Church.

How do I know we have nonbelievers in our worship services? Because there has been only one time in all those invitations when no one has made a public confession of faith. There have been some times when ten to fifteen people have responded in just one service. If we did not view our gathered worship services as a place for spiritually curious people, we would have missed many opportunities to share the gospel.[21]

Can we sing a new song? As a church seeks to reach people who are far from faith, we need to be willing to sacrifice our likes. When Russ and Marce visited Shoreline Church, they did not like the music. They had been around church for many decades, and the new music just did not connect with them. Still, we became friends with them and spent time with them in several social settings, growing to love them as a dear brother and sister in faith.

One Sunday, Russ and Marce came up to greet me after I preached.

Russ declared, "We're here!"

"Great," I said, "it's nice to have you visit again."

Russ looked confused. He clarified, "No, we're here, for good—this is our church now!"

Knowing how they felt about the music, I reminded him that we did not do many of the older, traditional songs.

Russ said, "We know, but we can learn to adjust to this style of music. What matters is that we feel led to this church."

Over the following years, this sweet couple discovered that God's glory, not our tastes, is central to worship. They learned to praise God with new songs and styles. They became faithful servants in our church community. Their heart for lost people grew, and they felt a freedom to invite others to church because it did not feel ancient and disconnected from the world where most nonbelievers live.[22]

From a funeral to a celebration. Does our worship feel more like a funeral or a party? Christians know that Christ is risen. The reason we meet each week is to celebrate that the Savior who died to pay the price for our sins rose from the grave. He conquered sin, death, hell, and the enemy. He has ascended and is alive and present today. This is worth celebrating!

Worship connects to outreach organically and naturally when Christians gather to encounter the living Savior. When we are compelled to sing from our hearts and declare his glory with passion, it honors God and draws lost people to him. As we worship the Lord during the flow of an ordinary day or when we gather with God's people on special occasions, the world can feel the Spirit, encounter the Savior, and hear the words of God speak light into the darkness. The world loves a party, so let's give them an invitation!

PART 4

Humble Service

How Caring Hearts and Compassionate Hands Show God's Love for All People

Jesus left the glory of heaven and came to serve us with his own life. His disciples joyfully serve their Savior, his church, and the world he loves. When we care like Jesus, the world sees a vision of the servant Savior and is willing to hear our stories of who Jesus is and how he loves.

CHAPTER 13

When God Knelt at Our Feet

It began in the heart of God and moved to the womb of a virgin girl. It was a dream of humble service that caused the angels to stand in awe of God's love for broken and sinful people. The Gospel of John tells us that "the Word became flesh and made his dwelling among us" (1:14). In Luke's Gospel, we encounter this baby born in a manger: Immanuel, God with us. God's plan to save his wayward children by humbly offering his own life began in the third chapter of Genesis. When our parents, Adam and Eve, took a bite of rebellion, and unity with God was shattered, Jesus knew what had to be done for our redemption. And centuries later, he took that step, becoming one of us to save us from the consequences of sin and restore our fractured relationship with God.

From his eternal preexistence, throughout his earthly life, and into all of eternity, our God is a servant. He is the King of all kings and the Lord of Glory, but his very nature is to humbly care for all creation and bring his wayward offspring home. Our God has the heart of a servant, and we see this frequently revealed through the life of Jesus.

When our Savior was drawing near the end of his life on this planet and preparing to go to the cross to exchange his life for ours, he gave us a powerful picture of service. Jesus gathered his disciples in the upper room of a house to celebrate the Passover. The bread and cup of communion were on the table in front of them, and in this special moment of remembrance, our Lord revealed the deepest part of his heart.

When God Knelt and Washed Feet

Imagine watching the angels of heaven as they saw Jesus scrub and dry the feet of his ragtag bunch of disciples. It was a shocking act of selfless love (John 13:1–11). A rabbi holding the feet of his followers and washing off the filth and muck of the city streets was unheard of. But what heaven saw and earth experienced was so much more than a popular rabbi breaking stereotypes. This was God in human flesh. The maker of heaven and earth, the divine Lord of the universe. Yahweh got on his knees and washed the feet of men too selfish to serve each other or him. As the men first entered the upper room, the bowl, pitcher of water, and towel were there for anyone to use. Yet each man walked past these instruments of service. Washing feet was a menial task reserved for servants, and none of them wanted to be identified that way. So it was Jesus who noticed and decided to take action.

To offer this act of service, Jesus had to kneel to touch their feet. The one who would feel nails piercing the flesh of his hands just a short time later took the feet of Judas the betrayer in his divine hands and gently washed and dried them. The God who spoke the heavens and earth into existence crouched at the feet of Thomas the doubter and cleaned between his toes. The one whom Peter declared the "Messiah, the Son of the living God" (Matt. 16:16), proved his messianic majesty as he explained to Peter what he was doing as he cleaned his feet (John 13:6–9). This was a precursor to the cross, where Jesus would soon wash the filth and sin from our souls. Jesus knelt at the feet of the Twelve one by one and served each of them.

A Yoke-Giving Lord

In a world of oppression, burdens, and discouragement, the servant God comes and offers to fit us with a yoke that does not crush us. As the son of a carpenter, it is likely that Jesus and his earthly adoptive father, Joseph, would have fashioned yokes. Much of the heavy lifting in the first century was done by beasts of burden wearing a yoke. If the yoke fit well, the animal could carry a bigger load. If the yoke did not fit, it chafed and the animal would be in pain and could carry less.

Jesus used this common image to describe one of the ways he serves his followers. Read these words with fresh eyes and imagine Jesus in the carpenter's shop carving and customizing yokes that fit just right. "Come to me, all you who are weary and burdened, and I will give you rest. Take my yoke upon you and learn from me, for I am gentle and humble in heart, and you will find rest for your souls. For my yoke is easy and my burden is light" (Matt. 11:28–30).

This is what Jesus wants to do for us as we walk with him. He wants us to carry the burden that is right for us. He does not want to crush us. Jesus, the servant, is still making yokes that fit his disciples just right.

Jesus' Mission

James and John, two of Jesus' disciples, along with their mother, made a bold request of Jesus one day. They thought it would be a good idea if Jesus reserved two thrones in heaven for them, the Zebedee brothers (Mark 10:35–40). Take note that this was not just a request for places of authority in glory, they wanted custom thrones directly next to Jesus, seated on his right and left. That is a reservation request! It's not just a table with a view but thrones right next to the Messiah.

After stating that they had no idea what they were asking, Jesus explained that worldly systems of government and power are not even remotely similar to God's ways. Jesus finished this teachable moment by reminding them (and us) about his purpose in coming. He said, "For even the Son of Man did not come to be served, but to serve, and to give his life as a ransom for many" (Mark 10:45). Jesus was emphatic: he did not come to be the recipient of service. His heart's desire was to serve others. His humble life would end in ransom, his life for ours. He took our shame, sin, guilt, and punishment into himself. In trade, we receive cleansing, freedom, healing, love, heaven, and the righteousness of God (2 Cor. 5:21).

A Surrendered Will

My way, my likes, and my desires fulfill *me!* This has been the unspoken mantra of every generation since Adam and Eve ate what was forbidden. Our servant leader, Jesus, lived with a radically different outlook. He existed to do the will of his Father. When his disciples wondered why he was not hungry, Jesus said that what truly satisfied him was doing the will of the Father (John 4:34). That was his food and sustenance.

After feeding five thousand people, Jesus explained that he is the bread of heaven and that his presence in our lives can fill and sustain us. Then the Lord of Glory declared that he came to earth "not to do my will but to do the will of him who sent me" (John 6:38). Jesus was consumed with the will of the Father, and it directed his thoughts and decisions.

We should be profoundly thankful that Jesus' servant heart was consumed with the will of the Father, because it led to our salvation. If you have never made the connection between Jesus' mission and your salvation, let these words of the Savior sink deep into your soul, and then pause to whisper a prayer of thanksgiving. Jesus said, "For I have come down from heaven not to do my will but to do the will of him who sent me. And this is the will of him who sent me, that I shall lose none of all those he has given me, but raise them up at the last day. For my Father's will is that everyone who looks to the Son and believes in him shall have eternal life, and I will raise them up at the last day" (John 6:38–40).

Our salvation, the assurance of resurrection, and eternity in glory are all set squarely on the shoulders of the one who came to humbly serve.

Serving through Healing

Jesus was drawn to those who were broken and in dismay. He did not move away from people with leprosy, as was the custom of the day, but he came near and touched them (Mark 1:41; Luke 5:13). The Lord served paralyzed people and they stood up and walked (Mark 2:11–12; John 5:8–9). The servant Savior gave hearing to the deaf and sight to the blind (Mark 7:34–35; Matt. 20:34). The dead breathed again at the word of Jesus the servant (Luke 8:49–55; John 11:38–44). The next time you read the four gospels, take note of how often the Lord served by extending a healing hand and meeting the deep need of a broken person.

Shackle Breaking

Jesus saw beyond the brokenness of bodies to the imprisonment of souls. Demonic powers were at work in the ancient world, as they are in every generation. When Jesus saw a person shackled, oppressed, or possessed by an evil spirit, he served them. At that moment, bread would not satisfy. Physical healing was not the greatest need. Deliverance was the longing of battered and spiritually tormented souls. It still is today.

Over and over, Jesus spoke with heavenly authority and chains fell to the ground (Luke 4:41; 6:18; 7:21; 8:38–39). Imagine the freedom and hope that were born in the heart of each person who encountered Jesus and said goodbye to demonic dominion in their life. This was so needed and so important to Jesus that he called his followers to serve the world in his name by entering this same kind of shackle-breaking ministry (Luke 9:1).

Final, Ultimate, and Radical Service

Foot washing is a powerful picture of humble service, and we can imagine ourselves mirroring our Savior with modern acts of foot washing. All the service offered by Jesus pales in the glory of the cross. The final and ultimate vision of service that should consume our souls and guide our lives is God on a cross.

Gasping for breath, in mind-piercing pain, with detractors glaring and mocking, and with the shame of our sin pounding down on his soul, Jesus hung for hours on a Roman cross. This instrument of torture was designed to display criminals for all the world to see. It was meant to be a slow and agonizing death. The guillotine and hanging are merciful compared with this ancient form of execution.

Most people focus on the physical pain of the cross, and it was unimaginable. But the spiritual torment and pain Jesus, the Suffering Servant, willingly took on himself were infinitely worse. Jesus felt our shame, he took the judgment for our sin, and the wrath we deserved was poured on the sinless Lamb of God. We can't comprehend what our Savior endured by his own choice for the people he had chosen.

More than three decades ago and a lifetime away, Sherry and I (Kevin) served together in youth ministry. A junior high girl who had just become a Jesus follower came to us troubled by the idea of Jesus hanging on the cross for her sins. She had grown to love the Savior, and the very thought of him suffering broke her tender young heart. She came to us with a theory. "I think I know what Jesus did. He was God, so he could do anything. I think, when he was on the cross, Jesus made it so he could not feel any pain."

It was clear why she had come up with this theory. We gently but clearly corrected her errant thinking. We explained that Jesus went to the cross willingly, knowing that he would suffer both physically and spiritually. We assured her that as Jesus hung on the cross, he knew her name, loved her, and bore all the pain, punishment, and judgment she deserved. Her eyes filled with tears of gratitude as we explained that her servant Savior felt what she would have felt had she been nailed to the cross being punished for her own sins.

It was not an act of cruelty to speak the truth to her. Jesus chose to take the cross, bear the shame, carry our sin, and give his life as the final and ultimate act of service. The very thought should break our hearts. What a wonderful servant Savior!

Serving while Dying

If we slow down and read the passion narratives reflectively, we will find Jesus extending specific and pointed service while dying for our sins. At the foot of the cross were his mother and John, the beloved disciple. It is inspiring to realize that while his body was being ravaged and his soul was bearing the full measure of our shame, Jesus served his mother and his friend. He knew that Mary would be unprotected. She lived in an ancient world with no welfare safety net, and so Jesus told Mary and John to look out for each other. In effect, he said, "John, take care of my mom." He told his mother, Mary, "Treat John like a son." (See John 19:25–27.) And John got the message. We read that he took Mary into his home to make sure she was cared for.

Most of us have a hard time serving others when we are feeling fine. It is difficult and sometimes impossible to serve others when we are sick. Jesus had nails driven through his wrists and feet, was hanging naked on a cross, and was bearing the punishment for the sins of every human being who would one day receive his death as a free gift. Yet even at that moment, he gasped out instructions to serve his mother and close friend. Again, Jesus shows us that he came not to be served but to serve.

Resurrection Did Not Change His Character

A quick little account appears near the end of John's Gospel. We can miss the power of it if we don't pay attention. Jesus had died on the cross. He had been buried for three days. He had risen in glory. In this time before his ascension, our risen Lord had many encounters with people. One of these was along the shore of the Sea of Galilee (John 21).

Some of the disciples had been out fishing all night and had caught nothing. Jesus appeared and called to them from the shore. After they admitted they had caught nothing, Jesus suggested they throw the net on the right side of the boat. When they did, so many fish rushed into the net that they could not pull it in. When Peter realized who was calling from the shore, he jumped into the water and swam for Jesus. When the rest of the disciples got to the shore with their net full of fish, they received an invitation from Jesus for breakfast.

If you have ever been out on the water for hours fishing, you know the glory and wonder of a warm meal. So get your mind and heart around this picture. The Lord of Glory, now the resurrected Son of God, had cooked some fish and bread for his friends. He knew they would be hungry. He would be teaching and instructing them. So the exalted and risen Messiah prepared breakfast. The weight of our sin and the grave had not changed his character. He was still a humble servant, willing to cook a meal for his friends.

But Wait, There's More

Have you ever watched one of those infomercials for some interesting product and during the pitch, the salesperson says, "Don't order yet, there's more!" They explain that if you order now, you will also get several spatulas, serving spoons, and other utensils with the purchase of your new nonstick pots and pans. They say something like, "That's not all! If you order now, along with your amazing vegetable slicer you get a bonus tool that makes radishes look like flowers." You get the point. Just when you think you are getting the deal of all deals, you find out there is even more.

Jesus' humble service began at creation when sin entered the world and God's rescue plan kicked off. It continued through God's work in choosing a family, then a nation, to bring about his promised King and Savior. And that promise was fulfilled when infinite divinity was placed in the womb of Mary, confined in human flesh. Jesus' humility was witnessed over and over as he walked on this planet and healed, set people free, washed feet, and served relentlessly. While hanging on a Roman cross and gasping for air, Jesus continued to serve as he looked out for his mother and a close friend. Even after the resurrection, the Lord of Glory took the role of host and prepared breakfast for some famished fishermen.

You might think that once Jesus ascended to heaven and took his rightful place on the throne of eternity, his service would stop. But wait, there's more! The exalted king of the universe is still serving us. In Romans 8, the apostle Paul tells us that the one who ascended to heaven and is seated at the right hand of the Father is still interceding for us. He can't stop serving! He won't! Our God is a foot-washing, cross-carrying, sin-erasing prayer partner who loves us beyond description and measurement.

Those who receive this servant Savior are called to be like him. We are to reflect his heart and character in all things. This is discipleship. We are to serve in ways that show heaven, the church, and the world that Jesus is still ready to serve any person who calls on his glorious name.

CHAPTER 14

Becoming Countercultural

Jesus' life was radically countercultural. Rabbis did not wash the feet of their disciples. Kings did not touch lepers. The demon possessed were consigned to graveyards and the outskirts of town, not invited over for dinner. The divine Son does not take on human flesh. God does not hang on a cross. The ruler of the universe does not come humbly as a servant. Jesus Christ broke every mold and then he called his disciples to do the same. Followers of the servant Savior live in ways that cause the world to scratch its head in stunned wonder. Signs of servanthood are all around us as we meet ordinary Christians who follow the teaching and example of Jesus.

Like a gift from heaven, a sweet couple named Jay and Lu offered to cover the cost for us to go to the Holy Land. This once-in-a-lifetime experience was an unimaginable gift of grace. On that trip, we met a wonderful couple who became dear friends, and for most of the tour, we hung out with Greg and Diane. We talked, learned, shed tears, and prayed together in places Jesus walked.

When we flew home to Michigan, we maintained a long-distance friendship with Greg and Diane. One day, this wonderful couple invited us to a Christian leaders gathering being held in

Jamaica. A devastating hurricane had hit the island country a short time before the event, but Greg and Diane contacted us to let us know that the hotel had weathered the storm and the event was still going to happen as planned. Over and over, the Jamaican people thanked all of us for coming. They explained that if the groups did not stay at the hotel and eat at the restaurants, they would simply shut down—and that meant no paycheck. We heard these words more than once: "We knew the Christians would come!"

Greg and Diane gave oversized tips to the people who worked at the hotel. They became friends with many of the staff, listened to their stories, and prayed with them. They also tried to find ways to serve these folks who had suffered so much. All of this was natural for them, like breathing. We were humbled by their desire to serve people they had never met and would probably not see again.

As we were getting ready to leave Jamaica, we discovered that Greg and Diane were not going home. They had met a sweet woman whose small house had been destroyed in the hurricane, and had learned that her kids were now exposed to the elements and that she had no money to rebuild. This loving Christian couple stayed behind not for a vacation but to serve. They spent their own time and money in sacrifice for another. And when they finally left Jamaica, the walls were up, a new roof was on that home, and this mother and her children had a safe place to live. As a glorious bonus, this sweet Jamaican family had seen a modern example of Jesus, the humble servant.

Not a Suggestion

Sometimes we misread the words of Jesus and don't get their full weight. When it comes to the spiritual growth marker of humble service, it seems that many of God's people have missed the message. Being a servant is not a subtle suggestion of our Savior. It is a bold command! It is one of the primary things that mark the life of a growing Jesus follower. In a dark world, humble service is a beacon of light that reveals the presence of Jesus and draws lost people to the heart of the Savior.

Just five days before our Lord shared the final Passover meal with his disciples, washing their feet and instituting communion, Jesus made his expectations clear. He said, "Whoever serves me must follow me; and where I am, my servant also will be. My Father will honor the one who serves me" (John 12:26). To follow Jesus is to fully embrace his mission of humble service. If we are going to be where Jesus is, we will care for the needy, hurting, forgotten, and broken in the world. When Jesus talked about his disciples serving others, nothing in his words or tone implied there was an opt-out program. To be a disciple is to serve like Jesus. Period. We serve in his name.

Just days after Jesus spoke the words recorded in John 12, he was sitting at the Passover meal. He had washed the disciples' feet with shocking humility. Then, when he returned to the table, Jesus looked at them and spoke. Read the Savior's words as if you are seated at the table and he has just washed your feet (because if you had been there, he would have). "'Do you understand what I have done for you?' he asked them. 'You call me "Teacher" and "Lord," and rightly so, for that is what I am. Now that I, your Lord and Teacher, have washed your feet, you also should wash one another's feet. I have set you an example that you should do as I have done for you. Very truly I tell you, no servant is greater than his master, nor is a messenger greater than the one who sent him. Now that you know these things, you will be blessed if you do them'" (John 13:12–17).

I have served you. Now you serve others. I have given you a clear example to follow. You call me Teacher, Lord, and Master, and that is who I am. This is serious stuff! To top it off, Jesus assured his followers that the true path to blessing comes as we serve others. Could Jesus have made it any clearer?

Watch Where You Sit

Jesus was deeply concerned that his followers be practical in the way they serve. When James and John came requesting the best seats in heaven, Jesus gave an emphatic no! This led to a lesson on servanthood and how Jesus put himself last (Mark 10:35–45). The religious leaders in Jesus' day had become masters at making sure they had the best seats in every situation. Prominence was their goal (Luke 11:43).

What a simple but profound lesson for Christians today! When you go to a gathering, don't walk in and look for the best spot. Instead, elevate others. Refuse to posture for power.

"Shotgun!" At sixteen years of age, that is what I (Kevin) always shouted whenever I was walking with a group of friends toward a car. There was an unspoken understanding that whoever called the front passenger seat first, got it. If I was not driving my sweet lime-green Opel Manta, I made sure I was lightning fast in calling shotgun. I certainly did not want to be stuck in the "way back" of the station wagon one of my friends had borrowed from his mom.

As I grew in faith and read the Bible, the conviction of the Holy Spirit settled into my heart. As odd as it may sound, I knew I had to stop yelling shotgun. Beyond that, I needed to willingly take the back seat. To force myself into a new lifestyle, I started yelling, "Back seat!" even though everything inside me wanted to yell shotgun. To be honest, a desire for the best seat still crops up in my heart more than four decades later. The battle continues!

Notice the Need

I (Sherry) love to hike. It is a wonderful way to spend time alone with God, so whether I am at home or traveling, I try to find time to walk around or find a hiking trail. While visiting New Zealand for

Organic Outreach ministry and a little time of refreshment, I found a nice hiking trail on Mount Maunganui near the quaint town of Tauranga. Late one afternoon, I went for a hike up the mount, and by the time I headed back, it was getting dark. As I was walking to our rental unit, I watched a lighted cruise ship making its way out of the port of Tauranga into the ocean. As the ship passed, I looked to my right, and to my surprise, I saw two elderly women lying on the ground at the bottom of a hill.

I ran to help them. They told me they had decided to watch the cruise ship, and one of them had fallen on the uneven ground. In an effort to help her friend, the other woman also fell. Once I helped them both up, I let them know I wanted to walk them back to their car. They told me they were fine and wanted to stay to watch the ship. For about fifteen minutes, I stood between these two sweet women, propping them up as we watched the ship sail away.

During our short time together, a friendship began. In our conversation, they shared their ages, eighty-four and eighty-seven. They appreciated the time I gave them and the care I provided, and I found myself encouraged to see these sweet ladies still having a fun adventure together. I took them to their car, and as I was helping the eighty-seven-year-old get in first, I felt the Holy Spirit nudge me to ask if I could pray for her. From our short conversation, I sensed that faith in God was not a part of her story. There was a pause, which confirmed my assessment. Then she sweetly agreed to let me care for her in this way. I prayed for her physical needs but also that she would know how much God loved her. I asked God to help her see that my finding them on the ground was a sign of his presence and care.

When I went to the other side of the car to help the other lady in, she gave me a hug and whispered in my ear, "Thank you so much for that prayer. I am a Christian too." As I was helping her into the car, she said, "You know, they always tell us at the home that if one of us falls, we should get help and not try to pick our friend up, lest we both fall." She smiled and said, "Thanks so much!"

I have found that one simple step in developing a heart and lifestyle of humble service is paying attention. When we keep our eyes open and listen for the Spirit, we'll find endless opportunities to serve in the name of Jesus. Humble service demands that we decrease our pace and increase our attentiveness. God provides daily opportunities for us to stop, care, help, and bless people through small and large acts of service. If we move too quickly, we may speed past divinely appointed service opportunities.[23]

Carry the Cross

Disciples hear the call of their Savior to deny self, pick up the cross, and follow Jesus (Matt. 16:24–25). Our Savior made it clear that if we will not live as cross carriers, we are not really Christ followers (Luke 14:27). Jesus' final act of humble service during his life was to bear his cross. In the ancient world, everyone knew that the cross was a picture of brutal torture and public shame. There was nothing attractive about it.

What does it mean to carry the cross? In the simplest words possible, it is to offer your whole life to God every day. To declare, "Jesus, I will die for you this day. I am yours—all of me." Imagine starting each day with this prayer: "Jesus, my servant Savior, you died for me. You served humbly to the point of giving your life as you took my sin and shame. I am yours today. All of me. I will do whatever you call me to do. I will go wherever you want me to go. I will love whoever you want me to love. I will die this day if it will fulfill your plan and bring you glory."

If every disciple started the day with this commitment, imagine how we could serve for the sake of our Lord. Washing feet would be done with ease. Helping the hurting would seem like the right thing. Carrying the load of others would feel light.

If we are ready to take up the cross, everything else will seem simple in comparison.

Serving Where We Live

For many of us, the hardest place to follow Jesus' example is where we live. When we get home, it is time to kick our feet up, relax with some media consumption, and let others do the heavy lifting. It is the private place where the world won't see whether we become a bit self-centered and demand some me time. No one is watching, right?

Wrong! If we have children and family in the home, they are tuned in to how our actions and stated beliefs line up. If we have roommates, they notice. If we live alone, we can know that our Savior still cares how we conduct ourselves behind closed doors. Followers of Jesus will hear his call to make our homes places of consistent, humble service.

Serving Where I Worship

It is possible to look at the church like a consumer. We can show up and expect a warm greeting, some coffee, a strong sermon, and music that fits our preferences. It is all too easy to look at our churches as vendors of Christian services rather than places to humbly serve our Lord, his people, and a hurting world.

Every follower of Jesus is gifted for ministry, and the Holy Spirit places one or more distinct giftings in us for the sake of edifying and strengthening his church (Romans 12; 1 Corinthians 12; Ephesians 4; 1 Peter 4). God calls us to discover, develop, and deploy these gifts. Humble service should begin in our homes, but it must extend to our spiritual homes and church families. If we are not engaged in meaningful service and investing our God-given abilities in the life of our churches, it is time to take a fresh new step and find a place to serve.

4 Generation Challenge (2-2-2)

When I (Sherry) was fourteen, my grandma (my dad's mom) had a massive stroke. Half of her body was ravaged. She never walked again, speaking was difficult, and navigating her home by herself was impossible. When this happened, I watched an example of humble service that has shaped my soul.

For the next eleven years, my dad and his siblings took care of their mother in her own home. She had served them for a lifetime. She had been a model of Jesus. Now they did the same for her. My grandma, Henrietta Vliem, had discipled her children in humble service through thousands of actions over a lifetime. Now my parents discipled me and my siblings as we watched them serve at great cost.

My aunt Phyllis went to Grandma's home every day for eleven years to help and care for her mom. They baked, laughed, and found delight in the things Grandma could still do. Aunt Gen took care of her on Sundays. After a long and hard day of work, my dad would come home, have dinner with our family, and then go to help his mother get ready for bed. He did this every night for more than a decade. Every other night, he slept in a small bed near his mom in case she needed anything. His brother, Larry, stayed with Grandma on the nights my dad was not there. Uncle Larry also helped early every morning. They shared the weight equally.

My mom and my aunt Marilyn gave up their husbands every other night for eleven years. That is humble service! In all those years, I never heard my mother or aunt complain once. Foot washing was a lifestyle.

If you are keeping track, my grandma served her children and taught them humble service as the way of a Christian. My parents lived this out and took her hand and the hands of their children. We learned to sacrifice and count the cost of Christian service by watching their example. That's three generations. Kevin and I have done our best to take the hands of our three sons, and now their wives, and model this same humble service. For more than thirty years, we have sought to make our home a laboratory of Christian growth, including humble service. You would have to ask our children how we have done so far. But our goal has been to engraft humble service as a lifestyle.

One of the greatest joys of our lives is watching our children with their children. At the writing of this book, our grandchildren are all younger than three years old. They are being well served by their parents. They might not know it yet, but our grandchildren are already being discipled to be humble servants. If you begin with my grandmother and continue to our grandchildren, you will see five generations of handholding discipleship in the area of humble service.

CHAPTER 15

Show Me Jesus and Then I'll Hear Your Story

Before I (Kevin) became a Christian, I had a vision of Jesus. I don't know how else to explain it. I saw a physical representation of the foot-washing servant Savior. He drove a VW Beetle and volunteered at a church in Garden Grove, California. I'm talking about a real, flesh-and-blood person named Doug. He had been a believer for only a couple of years, but Doug showed me that Jesus was real and still at work washing feet. I experienced God's grace through this young disciple before I became a follower of the Savior.

How did this college-aged, red-headed, afro-sporting wild man reveal the presence of the Lord of Glory? Simple. Through his humble service.

At the time, I was not old enough to have a driver's license, so Doug offered to drive me anywhere I wanted, anytime, if I could reach him on the phone. For younger readers, in those days, phones were all connected to a wire that was plugged into the wall. There were no phones that people could carry with them. But if I could catch him at home, Doug was willing to drive to where I was and take me where I wanted to go. Over and over, he drove fifteen to twenty minutes to where I lived, picked me up, dropped me where I requested, and then went home. The round trip could be up to an hour. When I wanted to return home, if I could reach him, he did the trip in reverse.

These were the pre-Uber days, and Doug never asked me to give him a single dollar for gas for all of those rides he gave me. As far as I can remember, I never offered to give him any money. My parents raised me better than that, but I was a self-centered, pagan surf punk, and it never crossed my mind to offer him any. Over and over, I called. Over and over, Doug served, never once complaining about my me-centered attitude.

While we drove, Doug asked questions about my life. He listened to my stories. And he talked with passion about what he loved. Sports, his girlfriend (whom he eventually married), and, above all, Jesus. While in Doug's brown VW Beetle, buzzing from point A to point B, I heard stories of grace, the power of God, Doug's radically changed life, and how much Jesus loved me. I met Jesus while getting a free ride to my girlfriend's house. One of the biggest doorways to organic outreach is humble service. It reveals the presence of Jesus.

Good Deeds Can Open the Door

Many churches and Christians believe that kind acts of humble service are all we need. There is no reason to verbally share the gospel when we can simply show God's love by serving others. They refer to this service by various names, often under the broader categories of outreach or evangelism. They believe that if Christians provide food, clothing, care, and help, they have shared the gospel.

But they are wrong. The apostle Peter calls all followers of Jesus to "always be prepared to give an answer to everyone who asks you to give the reason for the hope that you have. But do this with gentleness and respect" (1 Peter 3:15). The Bible is very clear on this: we must add words to our actions. We are called to point to the one who can give bread from heaven and not just food for this week. And we are to do this with a respectful attitude.

The church we serve has a great food pantry ministry. During 2020, the number of people we provided food for doubled and then doubled again. In the last quarter of that year, during the pandemic, our food pantry served 10,156 people. Through humble service, an amazing team of volunteers and staff gathered huge amounts of food, sorted it, bagged it, and handed it out to people in a time of great need. In addition to food, we had a team of prayer partners who asked every person or family who drove up, "Is there anything we can pray about for you?" More than 70 percent of the people, most of them not church attenders, said yes. This team prayed right then, recorded their need, and shared it with others so they could pray as well. When it was appropriate, these faithful servants also shared their personal stories. There was such a long line of cars that they had time to chat. Our prayer partners gave not only prayer but also a listening ear. They also offered free Bibles in English and Spanish. In each bag of food, we placed a printed invitation to church online or an outdoor service. We also provided information about children's and youth ministries. We offered physical bread and spiritual bread. We never forced prayer or spiritual conversations in our outreach ministries, but we always offered.

We have had this conversation, time after time, with church leaders all over the world. We understand that verbally sharing about Jesus is becoming increasingly unpopular in many places. But it is essential for us to add words about Jesus to our acts of service. Why? Because our good deeds are not enough to reveal the truth of Jesus. Only words of truth, infused by the Spirit of God, can do this. Think about it. Even the humblest acts of service, with no words or witness, will fail to reveal the truth of the gospel. Even Jesus, who was God in human flesh, added words to his service. How can we do any less?[24]

Our team at Organic Outreach International trains and works with church leaders all over the world. One pastor had been engaging in organic outreach for almost two years when this truth finally broke through in the hearts of some of the church volunteers. Two leaders of their church's homeless ministry were moved to seek forgiveness for how they had been leading. For years they had been showing up at a homeless camp with their team of volunteers to serve meals. Every week, they would stand on one side of a table, dishing out food onto plates. Not a single salvation had resulted from their countless hours of faithful service. Recognizing that there wasn't any spiritual component involved in just filling a plate with food, they had recently shifted things up, and after they were done filling plates, they would scatter among the tables and sit with those they had just served, building relationships and sharing the character of Jesus through stories and conversations. The confession was that in the past few months, since their shift from just serving to loving and sharing testimonies of God's grace, they had seen more than thirty individuals put their faith in Jesus Christ. These excited volunteers asked permission to start leading church services at the homeless camp. Needless to say, the pastor joyously gave his enthusiastic support for this new worship service and ministry. Their service continued, but their sharing of testimonies and the gospel transformed the ministry and bore eternal fruit.

Jesus made it clear that our good deeds should lead people to glorify God, not us. The Savior calls us to let our lights shine so people can see our good deeds and then give glory to the heavenly Father (Matt. 5:16). This happens only when we explain that we serve in Jesus' name and that ultimately he is the giver of the good gifts they are receiving. Humble service is not the end of evangelism, it is the door that opens the way to speak words of life, tell Jesus' story, and share the good news of the hope that is found in him alone.

When They Ask, "Why?"

As we learn to serve like the Savior, people become curious. The more self-centered our world grows, the more our humble service will stand out as unusual and countercultural. When people ask us why we serve as we do, and why we live with such care for others, we have a natural response. In the Gospel of Matthew, Jesus said that when we feed the hungry, give drink to the thirsty, extend hospitality to strangers, clothe the cold and naked, care for the sick, and visit people in prison, we are actually caring for him (Matt. 25:40–43). Every person is made in the image of God (Gen. 1:27). The creator of heaven and earth loves every human being so much that he gave his greatest gift to save them (John 3:16). God treasures each person, and he desires every one of them to come to faith in Jesus (2 Peter 3:9). That is good news!

I (Sherry) was boarding a plane to speak at a women's conference. I was looking forward to using the four-hour flight to review all of my notes for the three-day conference, in which I had several messages to give. I settled into my aisle seat, which I had secured in advance.

As the other passengers were boarding, a gentleman sitting four rows back began to make a request of all in his vicinity. He was loud and boisterous and asked anyone in an aisle seat to trade for his middle seat because he had a bum knee.

To be honest, when I heard his request, I didn't feel obligated to give him my prized seat, since I was a few seats ahead of him. I didn't even turn to look. But it wasn't long before I sensed the Holy Spirit's prompting. I wasn't aware of that prompting right away, but I was aware of an internal conversation. "God, I really need this time to prepare for my talks. Surely this is how I am serving you at this moment." Then I realized that God was prompting me to offer this man my seat and that I was trying to excuse myself for not giving it to him. With a raised hand, I motioned to the man that I would trade with him.

When I settled into my new seat, the gentleman next to me on the aisle asked, "Why in the world would you ever do that?"

I responded, "Do you really want to know?"

"Yeah," he replied.

"Well, honestly, the only reason I did it is because I am a Christian."

I so wish I could recall the string of adjectives he used to describe me. "Oh, you're one of those . . .," to which I replied, "Actually, no, I am a follower of Jesus trying to live out my life like he did."

He settled right down and began to ask me about my beliefs, starting with whether God sends people to hell if they don't believe in him. I had my Bible with me, so I asked his permission to show him some passages to help answer that question. I began with John 3:16–17. That first question led to a conversation that lasted the entire flight as he shared his struggles with faith and, really, all of life.

After the flight, as we were deboarding, I told him I would be praying for him to encounter Jesus. With a smile on his face, he looked at me and said, "Maybe I just did."

I was grateful for the Holy Spirit's leading to go to a place I would not have chosen and for an opportunity I otherwise would have missed to share God's message of love. You never know what adventure awaits you.

Make Your Home a Lighthouse

One of the best places to extend service is the place where you live. It doesn't matter whether you live in an apartment, on a military base, in a neighborhood, in a city, or out in the country, there are always people living somewhere near you. You might share a wall or have a few miles of farmland between you, but you have neighbors.

Ask the Holy Spirit to grow your love for those who live near you. Get to know their names and needs so you can pray specifically for them. Build friendships and find ways to offer humble service. If you are not sure where to start, a number of ministries have developed a simple pathway to being a good neighbor.[25]

Serving Where We Work

God has placed many of us around people on a daily basis. In a work environment, we can find many ways to serve and care, and this can open the way to spiritual conversations and give us a chance to point people to Jesus. A dear friend of our family is a doctor and serves many people every day. He believes their physical health is affected by their emotional, relational, mental, and spiritual health, so he seeks to treat the whole person. He takes time to talk with them, listen to their concerns and questions, and care for every aspect of their lives. When they share a need, a struggle, or a challenge in their lives, he often asks, "Would you like me to take a moment right now to pray for you?" Almost every person says yes. As you can imagine, this opens the door to deeper conversations. He works at a community hospital that has no religious affiliation, but he has never had pushback for offering prayer along with his medical expertise.

Another way we serve is by having a strong work ethic. Christians in any place of employment should be the most diligent workers. We should show up early, stay a few minutes late, and model excellence in all we do. We should never enter into gossip or office politics. Along with doing the best we can at our jobs, we should be quick to serve our fellow employees in the grace and power of Jesus. What an amazing privilege to work side by side with people who do not yet know the love of the Savior. May our acts of service and words of good news make our workplaces ministry centers.

Serving Where We Play

Hobbies, sports, gaming, social settings, free-time activities—these are all places we can serve in the name of Jesus. If we notice divinely appointed opportunities, our play time will take on new meaning. What could happen if we saw ourselves as servants where we play?

When Bill was a little boy, his family would take drives along the coast of Monterey Bay. He remembers his family stopping at a place called Point Joe, a beautiful outcropping of land in Pebble Beach which can be reached via 17-Mile Drive. No one in Bill's family played golf, and when they stopped at Point Joe, everyone would look with awe toward the beauty of the ocean. But Bill would turn his back to the ocean, look at the golf course, and say to himself, "I love this place, and I am going to play golf here someday!"

Decades later, after a lifetime working and serving as an optometrist, Bill retired. Guess where he moved? To Carmel, California, near Pebble Beach. His home is now minutes from Point Joe and the golf course. He and his wife, Sally, joined the golf club, and it became for them a place of play, fun, friendship, exercise, great dining, and humble service. This sweet couple has become friends with a large number of the members and many of the staff. From golf pros to groundskeepers to waitstaff, Bill and Sally love them all! We have been deeply moved watching this couple serve people where they play. We have seen them talk to members of the waitstaff and then pray over their needs. They care about the people there, they know their stories, and they prayerfully support them.

We believe that when Bill was a little boy, the Holy Spirit was whispering to him. Golf clubs (and all sorts of gathering places) need Christians who will humbly serve and extend the care, love, and message of Jesus. Many people may never darken the door of a church, but God sends his servants to shine the light of Jesus where they play.

Making Your Church a Service Center

How does your community view the church you attend? Do they see it as essential and needed? Are they amazed by the way your church serves?

When we moved to Monterey to serve at Shoreline Church, the church was getting ready to celebrate fifteen years of ministry. The founding pastor, Howie Hugo, was preparing the church to transition to a new lead pastor and a fresh season of ministry. As we spent time in the community around the peninsula, we found a recurring theme. People in that area knew about Shoreline Church. Christians from other churches liked Shoreline. Neutral nonbelievers spoke well of the church. Even hostile non-Christians who did not like churches in general had good things to say about Shoreline.

In our experience, this is not always true of a church. Some people view churches with suspicion or even resentment for not paying property taxes. So it was a bit shocking but encouraging to hear consistent and unsolicited positive feedback about the church. We soon figured out why people were so positive. They did not talk about the church's doctrine, although it was rock solid and orthodox. Folks we met did not rave about the preaching or the music, although both were strong. They were certainly not impressed by the beautiful building and lush facilities, because the church had just moved out of a tent and into a converted warehouse. So why were so many in the community positive about the church? You can probably guess. It was their long-standing record of humble service in the community.

People would say, "That's the church that loves our community." "They are the ones who feed hungry people." "That is the church that serves breakfast to everyone who comes, every Sunday morning, and they have great donuts!" "Shoreline is the church that goes to visit people in care facilities." "Aren't they the ones who give hundreds of backpacks filled with school supplies to underprivileged children?" The comments went on and on like this.

When people were in a time of loss, struggle, or spiritual searching, they sensed that Shoreline was a good and caring place with compassionate people. And they were right. When they came to visit, they also heard the good news of Jesus, and many of them have come to faith. If a church wants to reach their community, they must love passionately and serve consistently, and then they can share the story of the greatest servant who ever lived.

We can also be a witness to our community by serving other churches. If we want people to be drawn to Jesus and have an interest in attending a Christian church, we should love, bless, and partner with other congregations. As followers of Jesus, we have an enemy, but it is not other churches. We should see ourselves as partners with every Bible-believing, Jesus-following, community-loving Christian congregation. Let's pray for other churches, speak well of them, share resources, unify in serving our community, and show the world we are Christians by the way we love one another (John 13:35).

Radical and Shocking Service: Counting the Cost

Jesus calls his followers to serve at great cost and in ways that do not always make sense. In just a few verses, Jesus calls us to a level of sacrificial service that is hard to comprehend. Read these words as if Jesus is speaking to you: "You have heard that it was said, 'Eye for eye, and tooth for tooth.' But I tell you, do not resist an evil person. If anyone slaps you on the right cheek, turn to them the other cheek also. And if anyone wants to sue you and take your shirt, hand over your coat as well. If anyone forces you to go one mile, go with them two miles. Give to the one who asks you, and do not turn away from the one who wants to borrow from you" (Matt. 5:38–42).

What is Jesus saying? Are we to invite abuse and ignore dangerous behavior? Of course not! Instead, Jesus draws a radical and necessary contrast with the reflexive response we have when we are attacked. We are quick to defend ourselves or pay others back for what they have done, but Jesus wants his followers to be careful not to retaliate. Instead, we should pause in every situation and discern whether God could use our pain, our suffering, and our sacrifice for the sake of his gospel. If our sacrificial and humble service can advance the work of Jesus, there will be times we should willingly and voluntarily go the extra mile, give to one who asks, and turn the other cheek.

The apostle Paul also understood this delicate balance. There were times when he was arrested and suffered unthinkable abuse. Five times he was tied up and publicly scourged. This meant receiving what was called "the forty lashes less one." They had learned that forty lashes would kill a person, so they beat them within an inch of their life (2 Cor. 11:24). Paul carried 195 scars on his body that proved he was willing to suffer for the sake of the gospel.

When Paul was bringing the good news to the city of Philippi, a woman by the name of Lydia came to faith in Jesus and her whole family received the Savior. It was a mini revival. A short time later, Paul was arrested by officials, stripped, beaten with rods, severely flogged, and thrown in prison (Acts 16:22–24). At any moment in this series of abuses, Paul could have said, "I am a Roman citizen," and they would have stopped immediately, yet he remained silent. We might find it unbelievable that Paul didn't clarify his rights as a citizen, but it is clear that he sensed his circumstances were pregnant with evangelistic potential. He voluntarily accepted abuse for the sake of the gospel.

In the middle of that same night, while in prison and still in excruciating pain from being beaten, Paul and Silas were praying out loud and singing praise to God. Everyone in the jail was listening (Acts 16:25). After a divinely appointed earthquake set them free, Paul encountered his captor, but rather than let the prison guard kill himself because he thought his prisoners had escaped, Paul showed mercy and befriended the guard. He told him the good news of Jesus, and the jailer invited Paul into his home, fed him, and introduced his entire family to him. Another revival erupted, and the jailer's family put their faith in Jesus.

If Paul had claimed his privileges as a Roman citizen, he would not have been beaten and he might not have ended up in jail. Had he not been in jail, the guard and his family would not have heard the gospel and come to faith in Jesus. Could it be that Paul willingly suffered because he believed it would propel the message of Jesus? It certainly seems so.

Was Paul's willingness to suffer a blank check for people to abuse him? No, and we know this because there were other times when Paul said an emphatic no to suffering. Later in the book of Acts, we find Paul being attacked again. A crowd had turned against him, and he was imprisoned by the governing authorities. The commander ordered that Paul be flogged and interrogated, so the guards stretched him out and were about to begin the beating. At that moment, Paul could have remained silent, as he did in Philippi, but instead, he asked a question to which everyone knew the answer: "Is it legal for you to flog a Roman citizen who hasn't even been found guilty?" (Acts 22:25). At these words, the guards were alarmed and withdrew. Laying a hand on Paul was against the law because he was a Roman citizen by birth.

Why did Paul play the citizenship card at this moment? It appears that he had no direction from the Lord that taking this abuse would have redemptive results and lead anyone to salvation. With that in mind, he said no to the beating. At other times, it seems Paul knew his service of suffering would accomplish God's will and further the gospel. In these cases, Paul kept silent and suffered for his crucified Lord.

There are times today when we can choose to suffer for the gospel, turn the other cheek, go the extra mile, and give to those who ask. In a part of the world where there is persecution of Christians, a pastor was thrown in jail with no trial or explanation. He refused to complain, and started ministering to other prisoners. In a matter of days, he'd started a weekly church service and begun discipling some of the men in the prison. After three months, they decided to set him free. He asked if he could stay for a couple more months and finish establishing a church in the prison. They said no. But they gave him permission to come back weekly to work with prisoners, since what he was doing seemed to bring peace among the inmates.

It is unlikely that we will be beaten for our faith or thrown in prison. But we can decide to humbly accept suffering if we believe it will advance the cause of Jesus and spread his good news. How will you respond when you are overlooked for a raise or a new position at work simply because you refuse to cut corners or engage in "common practices" that could compromise your faith? Will you keep serving Jesus and seek to honor him when you are excluded from social circles because your faith is too bold and unbending? When you have a chance to speak up for what is good, right, and honoring to God, will you do it even if it could cost you something? If we pay attention, we can all find opportunities to be faithful to Jesus and shine his light, even when we know the price might be high.

If we sense that our suffering and sacrifice will have no kingdom impact and will not forward the cause of Jesus, we can say no. If we are convicted that the price we will pay could lift up Jesus, we can press forward. May the Spirit of God give us wisdom to know when radical service is exactly what is needed, whatever the cost.

PART 5

Joyful Generosity

*How Sharing Our Time, Resources, and
Abilities Captures the Attention of the World*

Jesus gave all he had and all he was for us. With divine generosity, he left glory, came to earth, took our sins, and died in our place. Now he calls his disciples to walk in his footsteps. As we give with generous and joy-filled hearts, the world can see a picture of God's love. Joyful generosity captures the attention of a world possessed by possessions.

CHAPTER 16

What More Could He Give?

Over the centuries, scholars have written thousands of pages all trying to explain one word in the Bible—the Greek word *kenosis* found in the great Christ hymn recorded in Philippians 2:7. Here is the full text of this ancient worship song celebrating the glory of Jesus:

> Who, being in very nature God,
>   did not consider equality with God something to be
> used to his own advantage;
> rather, he made himself nothing
>   by taking the very nature of a servant,
>   being made in human likeness.
> And being found in appearance as a man,
>   he humbled himself
>   by becoming obedient to death—
>   even death on a cross!
>
> Therefore God exalted him to the highest place
>   and gave him the name that is above every name,
> that at the name of Jesus every knee should bow,

in heaven and on earth and under the earth,
and every tongue acknowledge that Jesus Christ
is Lord,
to the glory of God the Father.

—Philippians 2:6–11

In the New International Version, the word *kenosis* is translated "made himself nothing." In the Revised Standard Version, it is "emptied himself." In the old King James Version, we read "made himself of no reputation." All of these translations are seeking to capture the meaning of this single word. The truth is that even if scholars used an ocean of ink, they could not fully explain what this word is attempting to signify, for it refers to what happened when the Son, the divine and eternal second person of the Trinity, left the glory of heaven and became a human being, giving himself to us and for us.

Jesus Gave Up

To understand the extent of the joyful and generous nature of our Savior, we have to pull back the veil of eternity and seek to comprehend what is not fully comprehensible to our limited understanding. As disciples of Jesus who want to be like him in every way, let's invite the Holy Spirit to give us a new and deeper vision of what the Son of God did when he left the glory of heaven and entered our world, becoming Jesus of Nazareth, the Jewish Messiah and savior of the world.

Jesus gave up his eternal home and moved into our neighborhood. For all eternity, our Lord Jesus, the divine Son of God, has been in perfect communion with his Father and the Holy Spirit. With his Father and the Spirit, he created this world and made heaven his home with the entire universe as his back porch. When the Son of God emptied himself, he did not cease being God. But he took on human nature, becoming subject to all of the limitations of our humanity. The one who spoke the heavens and earth into existence "emptied himself" of privilege and became a servant, Jesus of Nazareth, taking up residence in a small corner of his vast creation.

Jesus gave up angelic praise for human mocking. Ever since the dawn of creation, the Son of God had unceasingly heard, "Holy, holy, holy is the Lord God Almighty, who was, and is, and is to come" (Rev. 4:8). Heavenly beings beyond our imagination celebrated his glory, worshiped his majesty, and sang songs of praise in his name. Yet when Jesus willingly made himself nothing, he heard a new chorus. Religious leaders accused him of blasphemy. One of his closest friends cried out, "I don't know him. May I be cursed if I know Jesus." Roman guards joked, "If he really is a king, he could save himself." Heaven must have watched in stunned amazement that the Lord of glory would allow himself to be treated with such disdain.

Jesus gave up omnipresent being for the confines of a young girl's womb. Space and time cannot contain the Son of God. His being is infinite and eternal. When he gave himself for us, the boundless one was placed in the confines of a virgin womb—infinite being in a human embryo, the omnipresent Lord bound in human flesh. What wondrous love would lead the Son of God to pour himself out for us?

Jesus gave up omnipotent power for reliance on a newlywed couple. The Son of God is eternally almighty without limit. His words were the source of creation. His sustaining power keeps our little planet spinning on its axis and flying through space around the sun. When he willingly and joyfully became a man of no reputation, the Creator was subject to his creation. His source of nourishment was the milk of a young Jewish girl. His protectors were first-time parents who were on the run from an insane king who wanted their son dead. God Almighty was taught to walk, talk, read, and write.

Jesus gave up perfect wholeness for fractured brokenness. Peace, harmony, and trinitarian unity had been the joy-filled experience of the Son of God for all of eternity. When he emptied himself and was made in human likeness, he entered a broken and fractured world. He did not keep human pain and suffering at arm's length. Jesus embraced all of this. As the prophet Isaiah declared five centuries before the Son of God became incarnate, the Messiah would be wounded, afflicted, and bruised to make us whole (Isa. 53:4–5). Jesus experienced the full impact of betrayal by friends, he suffered physical torture, he was rejected by those he came to save, and he felt abandonment by his Father as God's judgment and wrath were poured out on him. What more could he give?

Jesus gave up the light of heaven for the darkness of death and the tomb. Jesus left behind the glory and light of heaven when he made himself nothing. He walked into our dark and sin-filled world. He felt the weight of infinite judgment and wrath when he took our sins on himself. He felt the dark hands of death squeeze the life out of him. Then the Lord of light was buried in a tomb for three days.

No Christian would question whether our Lord Jesus is the most generous being in the universe. What he gave up for us is beyond our wildest imagination. If we had a thousand lifetimes to serve Jesus, we could not begin to pay back what he gave when he emptied himself and took on flesh.

Jesus was infinitely generous. But was he still joyful while giving up so much? The writer of Hebrews answers that question with surprising clarity. Have you ever noticed these words recorded in our Bible? "Therefore, since we are surrounded by such a great cloud of witnesses, let us throw off everything that hinders and the sin that so easily entangles. And let us run with perseverance the race marked out for us, fixing our eyes on Jesus, the pioneer and perfecter of faith. For the joy set before him he endured the cross, scorning its shame, and sat down at the right hand of the throne of God. Consider him who endured such opposition from sinners, so that you will not grow weary and lose heart" (Heb. 12:1–3).

In this passage, we are called to run the race of faith with our eyes fixed on Jesus. He was born to die in our place and took upon himself the full shame of the cross—and he did it gladly. It was "for the joy set before him" that Jesus endured all he did.

Why is joyful generosity a marker of spiritual maturity in the life of a Jesus follower? Because it is what marked the life of our Lord. When we think of God's generous heart, let's refrain from making our primary focus the childish trinkets of this world. Has God been generous to you? If your mind first turns to the piles of material things that scream to be purchased, polished, and protected with insurance programs, you might not be thinking deeply enough. If your idea of God's generosity is measured by bank account balances, stock market movements, and worldly goods, think again.

The infinite God of the universe left glory and came to earth for you. He left behind angelic praise and heard crowds scream, "Crucify him!" In a mysterious act of sovereign grace, the eternal Son set aside his omnipotence to be born of a virgin girl. The light of heaven took the fullness of our shame and the wrath we deserved. He died in our place and was buried in the darkness of a tomb. "For the joy set before him he endured the cross." Let it sink in. "For the joy set before him he endured the cross." Has he been generous to you? "For the joy set before him he endured the cross." You are his joy. He endured the cross for you. Your Savior is joyfully generous, and what he has given should overflow from grateful disciples to the ends of the earth.

Giving as a Lifestyle

When we recognize all that Jesus gave in his incarnation, life, and death, we are inspired to live with ever-increasing joyful generosity. As we study the gospel accounts, we can learn from our Lord's example. By watching the ways Jesus was generous, we can get a vision of what our lives should look like.

Jesus had a generous heart like the Father. Jesus' model of joyful generosity was his Father. Again and again, the Savior told stories and used illustrations that pointed to the heart of the Father. In the well-known story of the prodigal son (Luke 15:11–32), we meet a father who was generous with both of his sons. When the younger brother took his inheritance and blew it on "wild living," he finally came to his senses and realized he could go home and live as a servant on his father's estate.

When his father saw him in the distance, he broke every cultural norm and ran to his boy, embraced him, and kissed him. Then he went over the top. He gave his rebel son the best robe in the house, a ring on his finger, sandals on his bare and dirty feet, and he threw a massive party. His lost son was home.

Many have written great books on this text, so we will focus on just one thought. Our God is joyfully generous! The father in this story is a mere shadow of our heavenly Father. When we turn to God and finally come home, his embrace and grace are waiting. He does not scorn us, shame us, or put us on probation. The amazing and generous grace of God is wrapped around us like a robe. All heaven celebrates and the party lasts for eternity. Jesus wants us to know that he and the Father are one and both are generous beyond measure.

Jesus gave what people needed. When the disciples asked Jesus to teach them to pray, one of the guidelines he gave was to ask God for daily bread—what we need (Matt. 6:11). In the Gospels, we see Jesus providing exactly this to the people he met who were in need. He supplied the basics of life: bread for the day, maybe some fish to go along with it. In all four gospels, we have a record of Jesus providing a simple meal like this in a miraculous way (Matt. 14:13–21; Mark 6:30–44; Luke 9:12–17; John 6:1–14).

Jesus knows what we need, and he always has a way of providing it, even if it isn't how we expect to receive it. We can make life complex and get caught up in the tsunami of wanting or acquiring more stuff, but Jesus gave us many warnings to help us be cautious about accumulating material goods. In many situations, what Jesus wants to give us are the simple necessities of life. He is joyfully generous in providing for our daily needs.

Jesus was lavish in his generosity. While in many situations our Lord provided the basic needs of life, sometimes he was lavish. When I (Sherry) think of the word *lavish*, Thanksgiving Day in my home as a child comes to mind. The holiday was special and memorable, and my parents made sure the focus was on gratitude to our Lord and Savior—along with great food. There was one dessert I looked forward to all year long. It was, and still is, pumpkin pie. I love it!

After a great meal with the family, it was time for dessert, so I would cut a nice piece of homemade pumpkin pie. Then I would take the Cool Whip out of the refrigerator. Notice I said refrigerator and not freezer. The Cool Whip cannot be hard or frozen; it needs to have softened in the refrigerator for the night. I would open up the Cool Whip container, stir it until it was smooth and creamy, and then spoon it on top of my slice of pie—spoonful after spoonful until the pie disappeared from sight. At that point, and only at that point, was this culinary delight ready for me to enjoy.

When I think of God's lavish generosity, I think of a fresh slice of homemade pumpkin pie totally covered in Cool Whip. That pie was lavishly covered, and God's generosity is like that—lavishly covering us. God's grace is lavish. His forgiveness is lavish. His love is lavish. The Scriptures speak of God's abundance of love toward us. "See what great love the Father has lavished on us, that we should be called children of God! And that is what we are!" (1 John 3:1). Take a moment to reflect on where and how you have experienced God's lavish love in your life.

When Jesus walked on this earth, there were several times when his provision went beyond what was needed. In the first recorded miracle in Jesus' ministry, our Savior turned water into wine at the wedding at Cana of Galilee (John 2:10). Not only did he miraculously transform six huge jars of water into wine, but it was so good that everyone could tell that Jesus' wine was superior to all that had been served up to that point. Lavish!

When Jesus fed the five thousand, everyone had enough bread and fish, and they all were satisfied. As a wonderful flourish, there were twelve extra baskets of bread (Matt. 14:20). Leftovers! Lavish!

When the resurrected Jesus met the disciples on the shore of the Sea of Galilee and told them to throw their net on the right side of the boat (after fishing all night and catching nothing), they did it (John 21:1–14). At that moment, the fish that had been avoiding them all rushed into the net. It was so full that they could not pull it into the boat. Lavish! When they got to the shore, they did what good fishermen do—they counted their fish. The Holy Word of God actually records the exact number: 153 fish! Can we say it together? "Lavish!"

Jesus was generous with his time. We all know time is precious, often more so than money or possessions. Jesus was a model of being joyfully generous with his time. Over and over, we read of people "interrupting" Jesus in the midst of his ministry, travel, or times of rest. Jesus never seemed to be irritated or bothered when this happened. He stopped what he was doing and gave his full attention.

On one occasion, Jesus was traveling with an influential religious leader. They were on the way to his home so that Jesus could heal his dying daughter. Along the way, a desperate and sick woman reached out and touched Jesus. She was hoping to go unnoticed. She was not trying to attract the attention of this great rabbi, just hoping to touch his garment to be healed and then watch Jesus continue on his way. But that was not our Savior's style. He wanted to see her face to face, so he stopped, called her over, and spoke unforgettable words of grace to her. "Daughter, your faith has healed you. Go in peace" (Luke 8:48). What powerful words! Daughter. Healed. Peace. You can't microwave intimacy. You can't race past people and love them well. Jesus gave his time to others, and he did it with a joy-filled and generous heart.

Our Savior affirmed generous giving. When Mary poured a pint of pure nard—a fragrant perfume worth several thousand dollars by today's standards—on the feet of the Savior, it seemed unnecessarily extravagant (John 12:1–8). Some said it was wasteful, that the perfume could have been sold and the money given to the poor. Jesus disagreed. There are times for sacrificial giving as an act of worship that brings glory and honor to Jesus. We might need to be careful about being too excessive in what we give to ourselves, but we can never be too generous toward our God.

Jesus commended proportional giving. Jesus celebrated when people were generous toward the things of God. He also made it clear that every single one of us can be generous. It is not about how much we have or give. What makes us generous is the level of our sacrifice. In a biblical story that lasts only four short verses, Jesus taught a significant lesson about generosity: "Jesus sat down opposite the place where the offerings were put and watched the crowd putting their money into the temple treasury. Many rich people threw in large amounts. But a poor widow came and put in two very small copper coins, worth only a few cents. Calling his disciples to him, Jesus said, 'Truly I tell you, this poor widow has put more into the treasury than all the others. They all gave out of their wealth; but she, out of her poverty, put in everything—all she had to live on'" (Mark 12:41–44).

What a powerful truth! We can be generous in any season of life and any financial situation. We give from what we have with joyful hearts and God is honored. As disciples, we watch Jesus, listen to his words, and follow his example. When we do this, he unleashes resources that can have a vast impact on the world around us.[26]

CHAPTER 17

The Adventure of a Generous Life

Joyful generosity is an essential and critical area of our spiritual maturity. There are many ways to be joyfully generous. Followers of Jesus can give of our time, and we addressed that topic in the section on humble service. We can be gracious with our words and bring blessing and encouragement to others through what we say. We will look at that feature of generosity in the next section of the book. We can give our whole lives to Jesus as faithful followers, and that topic is peppered all through this book. In this chapter, we will focus on growing in joyful generosity in the area of finances, material goods, and the stuff of this world. God has a lot to say about this throughout the Bible.

A Tale of Two Worlds

You might have figured out that the authors of this book come from dramatically different worlds. Many of Sherry's stories come out of home and family because of her godly upbringing. Kevin's personal history is radically different. We'd like to begin this chapter by sharing our journeys of growth in joyful generosity, contrasting our very different stories.

> **Kevin:** I grew up in a home with no overt faith except in science and self. My parents were generous toward people in need. It seemed we always had someone living in the room over our garage. My mom loved to volunteer and gave significant time to local causes. But we had no church affiliation, and I was never taught the value of giving toward the work of Jesus.

> **Sherry:** I watched my parents give the first tenth of all they earned to Fourth Reformed Church in Holland, Michigan. They did it with joy and humble devotion. My dad would cash his paycheck and put the first 10 percent in an envelope on top of the refrigerator. On Sunday morning, he would bring it to church and put it in the offering plate. In addition, my parents held the rest of what they had loosely and were willing to help people if they saw a need. In our home, generosity toward Jesus was viewed as a joyful privilege and part of our family life.

> **Kevin:** When I became a follower of Jesus, the idea of generosity was not on my radar. I read the Bible, but the theme of giving financially eluded me. I volunteered at the church with the youth ministry, but my limited money was mine! I had this sense that all of my life belonged to Jesus, but I did not make a real connection with that to my material goods.

> **Sherry:** As a young teenager, I modeled my giving after what I had seen my entire life. I gave God the first 10 percent of the money I earned at my summer and after-school jobs. I never thought about not giving a tithe. It was what you did as a follower of Jesus. I

loved and trusted my pastor and his wife and the leaders of our church and knew my giving was making a difference. I felt the weight, privilege, and joy of supporting the work of Jesus through my giving.

Kevin: When Sherry and I began talking about what our married life would look like, she raised the question of generosity. She asked about my practice of giving and whether I tithed to the work of Jesus. I tried out the deceptive line I had been using on myself for the past five years: "All I have belongs to Jesus! I have devoted my whole life to my Savior and his work."

Sherry: "That's great, but do you give of your finances? Do you set aside a portion of your income for the work of Jesus?"

Kevin: She was on to me! But I tried again, with a firm and obviously defensive tone. "I give everything to Jesus. I am completely sold out for him. I am going to become a pastor. All I have is his!" I thought that would do the trick and back her off. No such luck!

Sherry: "I know your devotion to Jesus, but do you actually give your money regularly, faithfully, and generously to the work of the church and the cause of Jesus?"

Kevin: I was cornered! The Holy Spirit used my sweet wife-to-be to make me look at my heart. I was hiding behind a lie. I could not say I had given all I am and all I have to Jesus and still keep every dime I made for myself. Sherry made it clear to me, with gentleness and kindness, that she loved me but was not interested in marrying a man who kept everything he earned for himself. This was a deal breaker for her.

Sherry: We talked and prayed about this topic for many hours in the following weeks. I walked Kevin through the lessons my parents had taught me about the privilege and honor of giving. We studied the Scriptures and grappled with the biblical teaching on tithing, generosity, and the dangers of greed.[27] By God's grace, our hearts aligned around the truth of God's Word, and we entered marriage with a commitment to give our first 10 percent to the work of whatever church we served and to leverage the rest of our resources in ways that glorified God and grew his work in the world.

The God who gave us everything expects us to give back. As followers of Jesus, when we read the Scriptures closely, we discover that our Lord modeled radical generosity. As his followers who seek to be like him, this should be enough to propel us into lives of freely sharing all we have. In addition, we know that "every good and perfect gift is from above, coming down from the Father of the heavenly lights" (James 1:17). All we have is given by the hand of our God. Jesus spoke to his followers with the clear expectation that they would live as consistent givers. In the Sermon on the Mount, Jesus said, "So when you give to the needy . . ." (Matt. 6:2). He goes on to give clarity about the spirit in which we should give, but the practice of consistent generosity is expected of those who seek to live like Jesus.

Any believer who says, "Jesus has all of me," but refuses to share their money and material goods is fooling themselves. If we want to be like our Lord and grow in Christlikeness, it is time to open our hearts and bank accounts. We need to invite the Holy Spirit into the vault that often stays locked and guarded from the church, people in need, and most of all, our heavenly Father, who gives every good gift.

God loves reflexive, spontaneous, and joyful giving. One man had spent his whole life earning and protecting his money. He was a master of manipulation and extortion. Like almost everyone in his

·chosen financial profession, he had become wealthy, and he'd done it on the backs of those around him.

Then he met Jesus. When he encountered the Savior, everything changed. God transformed his heart, and his finances followed. He had been protective of and obsessed with his wealth all his life. But in the light of Jesus' love and presence, he made a 180-degree turn. He tracked down every person he had cheated and gave back what he had taken, and more. Then he liquidated his assets and gave half of the money to the poor and needy in his community.

When we meet Jesus, really encounter him, he becomes Lord of everything in our lives, including our finances. If you are not sure you believe the details of this story, read it for yourself in Luke 19. Then ask Jesus to show his face to you with such clarity and beauty that you are moved to see everything you have as a gift from him. Ask the Holy Spirit to help you become so aware of God's amazing grace that your material goods pale in comparison. Invite your heavenly Father to make you so thankful for all he has given that you can't stop yourself from growing in generosity toward his work in the world and the people he loves.

Am I promised blessings if I give generously? Yes and no. Those who follow God and live in his ways will know amazing blessing. When we put our faith in Jesus and learn to give generously to his work, we are blessed beyond measure. But this blessing is not always financial. You may have heard religious hucksters promise that if you give $100 to their ministry, God will multiply it and surprise you with $1,000. Maybe they even had someone tell a story about how this happened to them. This kind of religious Ponzi scheme breaks God's heart.

The Bible does promise blessings when we give (Mal. 3:10; Luke 6:38), but those blessings can come in many forms. The joy of giving is a blessing in and of itself. Seeing God use our gifts to help others is a blessing. Health, family, church community, seeing the gospel go out into the world—these are all blessings. To reduce to dollars and cents the idea of being blessed is to minimize the glory of how God blesses his children. Sometimes, when we give a hundred dollars, what we have in our bank accounts is exactly one hundred dollars less. But we are always blessed when we give.

Warnings about Money, Stuff, and Being Rich

In his love, God often warns us. Like a compassionate parent, when our heavenly Father sees us running toward a cliff or into a busy street, he calls out. We are wise to listen to divine warnings, including ones about generosity.

Don't be a hoarder. How much stuff do I have? Do I really need it? Am I a hoarder? Sometimes we use the word *collector* as a cover for hoarding because it sounds nicer. It usually means that the things we hoard are more expensive and acceptable. But whenever we have more than we need and we keep adding to it, it's a sign that something might be wrong. Jesus told stories of hoarders (Luke 12:13–21), and he was clearly not a fan of this practice. What might happen if we evaluated all we have, prayerfully determined what God intends for us to keep, and placed the rest in open hands, ready to share as the Holy Spirit leads? How many might be blessed, and how might the world be changed by our generosity?

Don't let money be your master. Jesus issued this warning with laserlike precision. "You cannot serve both God and money" (Matt. 6:24). What drives us through a normal day? The will of God, or the pursuit of stuff? Where do our minds wander in our free time? Toward the goodness of God, or toward the next acquisition, vacation, or trinket we plan to purchase? What wakes us up and moves us into our day? An unquenchable longing to serve Jesus, or the need to make more money and acquire one more toy? The answers to these questions will help us determine what master has our allegiance.

As we reflect on the power of possessions and the lure of things, it is helpful to expand our thinking and recognize that more money is not always the driving force behind material enticements. Often there are idols behind the scenes that drive us to accumulate more. It might be that we are moved by a desire for pleasure. We could be seeking comfort in things. Sometimes a need for control or security is what keeps us buying and collecting. Materialism has many children, and we are wise to name them so we can resist them as well.

Don't love money and the stuff it can buy. The Bible does not say that "money is the root of evil." What it says is, "The love of money is a root of all kinds of evil" (1 Tim. 6:10). Years ago, the game show *Wheel of Fortune* wrongly used a shortened version of this sentence, excluding the beginning phrase, "the love of," for one of their word puzzles. They were flooded with calls to correct their error. The question is not do I have money, but does it have me? Has money become a lover that demands my attention, devotion, and heart? When this happens, we wander into the dangerous territory of idolatry. Every follower of Jesus should check their heart, regularly, to make sure they have not entered a love affair with the stuff of this world.

Don't make wealth your life's goal. Jesus encountered a man who was very religious and attentive to following the commands of God (Matt. 19:16–30). He asked the Savior what he needed to do to gain eternal life. Jesus gave a quick review of some of the Ten Commandments that relate to how we conduct ourselves in this world. The man said, "Check, check, check, check, check, check! I'm all good." Jesus then focused on the one command that plagued this man's soul: do not covet. The Lord Jesus, who had given this man all he owned, including his mind, talents, and strength, told him to be generous with worldly goods and focus on heavenly treasures instead. The man left Jesus sad, unwilling to share what God had given him. His life orbited the sun of worldly wealth, and he was not willing to change to let God be the center of his life.

Don't say, "Mine, mine, mine!" How we think and what we say are powerful. Over and over, the Scriptures remind us that all we have is a gift and that ultimately everything belongs to God (James 1:17; Ps. 24:1). How might our actions and attitudes change if we referred to everything as belonging to God and not to us? Seek to pay attention to how you speak about the money and possessions God has placed in your care. If you use "my" and "mine" a lot, make a shift to "God's stuff"!

Beware the power of debt. The Bible speaks clearly and repeatedly against being in debt (Rom. 13:8; Prov. 22:7). It is a form of slavery. The more we are in debt, the less free we are to live generous lives. The greater our debt, the tougher it is to live with joy. If you are in debt, commit to doing everything you can to get out as soon as possible.

A counterintuitive reality is buried in the principle of generosity: you will get out of debt faster if you start being generous now. Ask God for his power to give to others and commit to honor him by living within your means. Begin giving something, no matter how small it might seem, toward Jesus' work. Attack debt like the powerful and demonic enemy it is. In addition, read one of the books or follow one of the programs we recommend in the endnotes.[28]

Steps into Joyful Generosity

As a married couple, we have been learning to live and grow in the spiritual marker of joyful generosity for almost four decades. Along the way, we have discovered that this is a very important part of our discipleship journey. It is a day-by-day, step-by-step adventure. As you seek to fully follow Jesus in this area of your spiritual life, here are some ideas to help propel you in the power of the Holy Spirit.

Give to God first. In our early years of marriage, if we did not give to God first, we never would have given anything. Our income was $900 a month, so we wrote a check for $90 to New Hope Church every thirty days. We did this before we paid any bills.

Yet somehow we always ended up with enough for each month. If we don't give to God first, there is a good chance we will end up spending everything on ourselves.

Respond to divine promptings. Along with a regular rhythm of giving weekly, biweekly, or monthly, Jesus followers should keep their eyes open for needs and their hearts open to nudges of the Spirit. When we believe that God is whispering or speaking loudly and calling us to give, we should respond.

If you are worried that a prompting to be generous is not from God, stop to consider the other options. Could Satan be trying to get us to give finances to our churches or help a poor person? Not likely! Could it be that our altruistic and overly gracious selves want to give away stuff? Again, unlikely! So take a chance and be generous. If we give away more than we should, God is able to give it back.

When we were newlyweds and taking classes in seminary, we were blessed, but we were also broke. We didn't draw attention to our needs, but there was clearly no way we could both stay in school and live on my (Kevin's) ministry income. We prayed a lot and worried some too. We were struggling to make ends meet when one day there was a knock on the door. When I opened it, I saw Marc standing there, one of the guys I had met years earlier when I worked at Munchie's Pizza. We had become friends, and over time he had become a follower of Jesus. Though we maintained our friendship over the years, we no longer saw each other very often and had not talked for a couple of months.

I invited him in, and Sherry joined us as we sat down to talk. Marc was always a guy who got right to the point, so he looked at us and said, "This morning I was reading my Bible and talking to Jesus. He told me you need money. So I got on my motorcycle and came here." He handed us an envelope with cash in it. We opened it, and it was such a generous amount that both Sherry and I began to weep.

How could he have known? At that moment, we realized that our heavenly Father had whispered to one of his children, "Be generous," and he had responded!

Marc continued, "I'll be giving you that same amount every month until you are done with school." We were on the receiving end of joyful generosity, and it touched us deeply knowing that God cared about our needs and that we had a brother in Christ who was generous like Jesus. Since that day, we have tried to respond every time the Spirit of God calls one or both of us to be generous. When we do, God always shows up!

Invest in eternity. Jesus made it clear that there are two investment strategies. We can pour our resources into the things of this world, and they will rust and turn to dust. Or we can invest in what is eternal (Matt. 6:19–20). You know the old saying, "You can't take it with you." In a way, it's wrong. We can take the goods of this world and invest them in people. We can use our resources to reach the lost and see them come to faith in Jesus. When we do this, we are investing in eternity.

Check your heart. After telling his followers to store up treasure in heaven, Jesus wraps up his teaching by saying, "For where your treasure is, there your heart will be also" (Matt. 6:21). We need to ask, where is my heart? The only way to answer that question is to honestly and consistently identify what we treasure most. If it is stuff and the things of this world, we have our answer. If it is the glory of God, the mission of Jesus, and investing in the lives of people, we have a better answer.

Enjoy and celebrate what God has given you. God delights when his children enjoy his good gifts (Eccl. 5:19; 1 Tim. 6:17). We have a friend who believes this and lives it out in an interesting way. He sets aside the first 10 percent he earns to give toward the work of Jesus. Then he sets aside another portion of his monthly income for celebration and for blessing other people. Every so often, he plans something special, invites others to participate, and picks up the tab. When he does, he is quick to point to God's goodness and provision, which make it possible for him to live generously. What a beautiful source of encouragement and inspiration!

Grow in contentment. I am happy with what I have. If I had nothing more, I would be content and at peace. I don't need anything else to make me complete. Can you repeat these three statements and sincerely mean them? When we learn the secret of contentment, we live in freedom and joy. If we are always seeking more and believe we will finally be happy when we acquire the next possession, upgrade, or raise, we will never find true contentment.

God calls us to live this way for our own good (1 Tim. 6:6–10). He does not want us going through each day chasing a carrot hanging on a string just out of our reach. Here is the amazing secret many people never learn: If you are content today, exactly where you are, you will remain content if you have more or have less. In the same way, if you are discontent today, you will not be content if you get more. Contentment is based not on what we have but on living joyfully and thankfully with what we have.

Develop a habit of giving stuff away. If you are ready to go even deeper into the adventure of joyful generosity, develop a habit of giving things away. Look for reasons to share what you have. Notice when you have extra of something and another person has none, and have fun giving them one of yours. Walk around your apartment, house, or trailer, take note of things you rarely use and get creative as you think of people who would really appreciate them. Liquidate some of your assets and put that money to work for some church project or mission organization, or help a family in your community that needs a financial boost and a touch of love from the hand of God.

A few years ago, our oldest son and his wife accepted a challenge that involved giving things away every day for a month. Here's the catch. The number of things you give increases as the month progresses. On day one, you give away one thing, then on day two, you give two things away. By the last day, you are giving away thirty items. Our son and his wife were fairly new in their marriage and they lived simply. It did not appear as if they had a lot of extra stuff, but at the end of the month, they told us they'd had plenty to give away. They said it was good for them and they learned a lot in the process. They inspired us, so we did the same thing and found the experience to be very freeing. I would challenge you to consider doing this as well, as a practical step you can take after reading this chapter. And take it one step farther. When you choose each item, thank God for his provision and generosity to you, and then pray that it will be a blessing to the next person who receives it.

Here is one warning to avoid short-circuiting the blessing of giving. If you start giving things away, don't make it an excuse to get new stuff. Decide to live more simply. Become more grateful. And let your acts of joyful generosity connect you more closely to your infinitely generous Lord.

4 Generation Challenge (2-2-2)

As we grow in generosity, we should always take the hand of someone who inspires and challenges us to become more mature in the area of giving. We can let them disciple us and help us look more like Jesus in how we relate to material stuff. At the same time, we should lock hands with someone who needs to grow in this area. We can invite the Spirit of God to use us to help them grow more generous and joyful. We can even teach that person to do the same with someone else. That is the model we learn in 2 Timothy 2:2.

Jay and Lucille became like family to us. They were part of the church we served in Michigan, and once a year, they invited us to their cottage for a full day of fun, rest, and play. It was a highlight in our summer! Once, when we sat down for lunch, I (Sherry) noticed a wonderful and generous thing that Lu did each time we came. She had a cooler filled with drinks, and she told the boys, "Help yourself!" There were fruit drinks, sodas, and just about every beverage you could imagine a kid enjoying. It hit me that she went out and thoughtfully spent their money to find options our kids would love. It was lavish! I learned about simple and creative generosity by watching Jay and Lu bless us with their home, beverages, time, and resources.

I have followed this example. It does not cost a lot of money, but it does cost something. When we have company over, and especially if they have kids, I think about options that will be appreciated and will bless those who visit us. If people stay in our home for a few days, I take a page out of the Lucille Patmos discipling playbook and provide breakfast options, and I make sure there is plenty in the fridge that everyone will enjoy.

Over the years, many of our guests have thanked us for this spirit of hospitality and have mentioned how much it meant to them. We tell them that we believe God has provided for us so that we can be a blessing, show hospitality, and refresh those who come into our home. Now many of them are seeking to do what Lu taught me and what I have shared with them. I pray their example will impact a generation after them to be joyfully generous both with the little things of life (like an assortment of drinks) and with the big things.

Will you let someone take your hand and lead you to a whole new level of commitment in joyful generosity? And will you commit to doing the same for someone God has placed in your life? That is the journey of a disciple!

CHAPTER 18

Generosity Reveals the Presence of Jesus in Our Lives and in the World

A Christian can sing praise songs like an angel, read the Bible with scholarly attention, and pray with monklike devotion, and the world might not really notice or care. That's what religious people are supposed to do. If you want to get the attention of a self-centered and materialistic world, learn to be generous. If you really want to turn heads, be generous with authentic joy. Many people don't even have a category for a person who lives with joyful generosity.

Why do most people feel affection for their grandparents? Because grandparents love to give stuff to their grandchildren. They are joyfully generous.

When we are free from the power of consumerism and view all we have as a gift from God, generosity flows. When Christians leverage their resources for the sake of the world, people will be stunned. As we find growing delight in sharing what we have with those who are in need, God will use our generosity to draw people to himself and change the world.

A church with resources can serve their community. When God's people consistently give to their church, ministry to the community can flow. Too many churches are struggling to make ends meet, but churches should be conduits of God's provision for the needy in their communities. If every believer who has a church home gave regularly and generously, the potential for outreach would be staggering. The church would have ample resources to share.

Search your heart. Evaluate your lifestyle. Scrutinize your giving habits. Seek to be joyful in the process. It is easy to get defensive when it comes to our money and stuff, but Jesus is our perfect example. He held nothing back. If our hearts belong to the Savior, so will all the stuff he places in our hands. One of the best ways to invest in eternity is by giving to the ministry of the church family God has adopted you into.

What if everyone gave like I do? Ask yourself this question and let the Holy Spirit speak truth to you. What if every Christian gave with the same generosity and attitude that you do? Would this be good for the church? Would it propel the work of Jesus outward to the world?

If you can honestly say that the cause of Jesus would be strengthened if everyone gave just like you do, take a moment to celebrate right now. Give God thanks for your spiritual growth and for how he is using the resources you share to bring glory to Jesus. If you know that the work of the church would come to a screeching halt if everyone gave like you do, let the conviction of the Spirit fall on your heart. Repent. Confess your need to grow in this area of your spiritual life. Ask God to help you begin giving today (not tomorrow). And commit to keep taking steps in generosity for the sake of God's glory, the spread of the gospel, and your spiritual growth.

When we give to ministries, we have a voice. Along with giving to our churches, followers of Jesus who are maturing in the marker of joyful generosity should seek to support ministries that help people in need. When we do, it gives believers a voice in the lives of the people who are impacted by our giving.

Organizations like Compassion International care for children in need all over the world. When Christians give monthly support to groups like this, they provide education, food, and medical care, and open doors for the gospel. There is a specific way our giving can impact people when we partner with a ministry that does child sponsorships like Compassion. We can write letters to these children. We can extend hope, faith, truth, and life into their little hearts.

Now it's confession time. I (Kevin) am a bit of a skeptic and a cynic, and for several years, I was skeptical of several of the ministries we gave to and of how they were using the money we sent. For years, we supported children and wrote a check every month. We prayed faithfully for the kids we sponsored. But honestly, I did not really believe our support was going to those exact kids. I figured the money was all placed in a big pot and all the kids were taken care of the same no matter what was donated. We gave because we believed in the cause, but for years, I never wrote letters to the kids. I did not feel a real connection with them because I did not believe we were truly the only sponsors these children had.

Then I went with a team to El Salvador to do some Organic Outreach training with pastors. They told us we would get to meet some kids in the area who were sponsored by members of our church, and it just so happened that Juan, a boy we were supporting and continue to support, lived in that community. They said I could spend time with him, meet his family, and even visit his home. I looked forward to it, but the truth that I was his sponsor had not yet pierced my heart.

When I met this little boy, I discovered that he had only one sponsor—the Harney family. I asked one of the leaders, "Do all the children get letters?" She said, "Only if their sponsor sends them." I was shocked. It turns out that Sherry and I were not, as I secretly and cynically suspected, receiving computer-generated form letters written as if they were from Juan. Every picture sent was drawn by him. The list of favorite things he sent to us was his real list of dreams and loves. When the letter said, "Thank you for being my sponsor. I love you," these were Juan's words. And the little boy who never got letters from his sponsor was now sitting in front of me. It broke me, and I wept, and I don't cry easily. I had been giving my money, but now I was ready to give my heart.

Since that time, we have written letters and invested ourselves wholeheartedly in these children's lives. We tell them about our family, our loves, our church, and most of all Jesus. We encourage them to pray and seek God. We follow the guidelines set by the organization, but we have the privilege of helping these kids walk toward Jesus. We are seeking to take their hand and help them forward in faith. The act of generosity opens the door to share the gospel in the lives of these children and disciple them.

Generous acts invite God's presence and help people see Jesus. Every time a follower of Jesus is generous in our selfish world, we show the heart of our God. If people are stunned or surprised by someone who gives with contagious joy, it opens the door for spiritual conversations.

"Why do you give the way you do? Don't you care about money?" "You are always quick to give to others. Why are you like that?" Whatever the question, we have an answer. We follow a Savior who gave us everything. Through faith in Jesus, we are promised we are blessed "in the heavenly realms with every spiritual blessing" (Eph. 1:3). We have heaven as our home and eternity secured by the generosity of God. How can we not be generous?

When we are generous and joyful in the process, people will see Jesus in us. They will ask questions. We can share our stories of God's goodness and provision. As we mature in this marker of growth, God will open doors for the gospel that might not open any other way.

I had a funny experience when God opened the door for a new friendship, then spiritual conversations, and finally my new friend became a Christian. And it all came from my trying to give the government $25.

I had shown up for jury duty and spent half of my Monday at the court. When they released us, they said that we were done for the week. The woman who gave us the final instructions explained that we could pick up a voucher for our time and some of our gas costs. I raised my hand and asked if I could sign the voucher back to the county. I figured they needed the money more than I did.

As I walked out, a guy named Bill came up to me and said, "Why in the world would you give money back to the government?" This led to a brief chat where I told him that I really don't care that much about money. He was shocked, but intrigued. I told him that I already have everything that really matters in life. Now he was even more interested. When he asked me what I meant, I told him about all that Jesus had given me and done for me. I assured him, "I am infinitely rich!" He found this fascinating and asked if we could talk more.

This led to a weekly breakfast at a restaurant. We talked about life, business, and what it means to follow Jesus. Eventually, Bill decided he wanted to know the Savior and receive the grace of Jesus. One morning, over breakfast, Bill became my brother in faith as he prayed to receive Jesus. A simple act of joyful generosity at a court building opened the door for a friendship and eventually for Bill to hear and receive the gospel.

Self-centered lives compromise our witness to the God who gave everything. In the same way that generosity opens doors for the gospel, a self-centered life that fixates on the accumulation and consumption of stuff slams the door shut. The life of a disciple is meant to reflect the Lord we follow. How can we show Jesus to the world when our first love is money and the things of the world? What message do we send when selfishness drives our decisions and corrupts our motives?

Nonbelievers don't have a clear picture of what a Christian is supposed to be like. But they do have a sense of what we should not be. Selfish is near the top of that unspoken but commonly held list. Plenty of people do not follow Jesus or acknowledge him as Savior. But these same people have a sense that Jesus was good, kind, gracious, and generous. They expect people who bear the name of Christ to be like the one they claim to follow.

Giving shows the world we are not owned by things. So many people in our culture are mired in debt and consumed with consumption. Inside the church and outside, there are lots of people whose driving force is making money, acquiring things, maintaining what they own, and upgrading their lifestyle. This is a kind of bondage to the things we think we own.

When we are free from the entanglements of consumerism, and when we use what we have to be a blessing to others, we send a powerful message. We are not slaves. We are not in bondage. We are not driven by the need to acquire more and more.

The world watches Christians. People want to know whether there is a pathway and lifestyle that allow them to breathe easy, relax, and enjoy each day. If we live free from the entanglements of possessions, people will want what we have. Then we can tell them about the one who has satisfied our souls, provided for our needs, and given us inheritances in heaven that can never be taken away.

PART 6

Consistent Community

The Power of Togetherness in a Polarized World

G od exists in eternal perfect trinitarian community. Jesus made relationships a priority when he walked on this earth, and he called his disciples to live in consistent loving community. When we walk in loving fellowship with God and each other, the world will see that we have what their hearts long for. This draws people toward the only one who can heal their hearts, bind their wounds, and satisfy their hunger to belong.

CHAPTER 19

God Needed Nothing, but He Invited Us to Be His Friends

Glass swans. Gravy pitchers. Sports memorabilia. Old books. Vintage T-shirts. What do you give the person who has everything? It is a strange question that is asked only in wealthy cultures and among people who have so many resources that they can acquire more than they need and even more than they want. So they start collecting things. In some cases, they begin a collection so people will have something to buy them at Christmas and on birthdays. It is tough to give something to a person who has everything!

What do you give to the God who made everything, who rules the universe, and who is all-powerful? What does God Almighty long for? What can you offer to the one who is eternally self-contained and without need? Is there anything you can offer to the perfect trinitarian being who has existed in unspoiled community for eternity? The answer is yes. You can give yourself!

In a real and theological sense, God has no need. Theologians have written volumes on God's nature, sovereignty, and immutability (unchangeable nature), and on the reality that our Creator lacks nothing. Yet in some mysterious and incomprehensible way, our heavenly Father wants relationship with his children. The maker of heaven and earth longs to connect with his created ones. The sovereign Lord of eternity delights to call us friends.

Discipleship is about becoming more and more like Jesus. Our Lord loved community and revealed the heart of the Father when it comes to relationships. If we want to know how to grow in spiritual maturity, we can look to God incarnate, the Messiah, Jesus of Nazareth.

Jesus called people to follow him and be with him. In the early church, there were some groups who could not comprehend God's taking on flesh and becoming human. They did not believe he existed as God walking among us. Docetism was an early heresy that imagined Jesus as appearing to be human but not truly living in the flesh. Docetists were known for saying things like, "Jesus left no footprints." The idea was that he only appeared to be a man in a body, but really he was a spirit. Everything in the Gospels dictates against this kind of thinking.

Jesus walked along the Sea of Galilee one day, leaving real footprints behind him. This was God in human flesh, fully divine yet fully man. On this particular walk, Jesus encountered two men, Peter and Andrew. They were at work doing what they did almost every day, casting a net into the water. Jesus extended an invitation to them: "Come, follow me" (Matt. 4:19). Immediately these two men dropped their nets and upended their lives. They followed the rabbi, Jesus. A little farther down the shore, the Lord saw two more brothers, James and John. They were in the same line of work. When Jesus called out to them, they left their trade, their father, and their secure life to follow the Lord. His band of disciples was growing.

While traveling, Jesus met a tax collector named Matthew and extended him the same invitation: "Follow me" (Matt. 9:9). And he did! The next thing we see, Jesus was in the home of this man, who was hated and despised by the Jewish people. Tax collectors were known as traitors, thieves, and extortionists. Yet Jesus honored

Matthew by stepping into his life, meeting his friends, and sharing table fellowship. The level of intimacy was so profound that the religious leaders had no category for this behavior, except to declare it wrong.

The gospel accounts tell the story of Jesus' traveling with this group of disciples, sharing meals with them, teaching them, giving them a mission, and so much more. Nothing in the four biblical biographies of Jesus even hints at the idea that our Savior was a disembodied spirit appearing to be a real person. Jesus called the disciples to be with him and share life in all of its glory and pain. He invited his followers to experience the pedestrian and sublime. The disciples walked in Jesus' steps, and they could see every footprint he left.

Jesus called people to his mission. Following Jesus is more than just hanging out. Yes, the disciples were with Jesus for three years and shared an array of experiences, but there was a purpose embedded in all that Jesus did. When he called Peter and Andrew, he presented the reason upfront: "I will send you out to fish for people" (Matt. 4:19). What he meant by this unfolded in the years to come as they listened to his teaching, observed his life, grieved at his death, and gloried in his resurrection. His postresurrection teaching added the final flourish and gave them undeniable direction (Matt. 28:18–20; Acts 1:7–8). Fishing for people had similarities to fishing for fish, but it was radically different.

The disciples were called to go into all the world and share the message of the hope, life, cleansing, and meaning that come through Jesus, the Christ. The first followers of the Savior walked with him so that they could learn the truth of the good news. The perfect holy God who made the heavens and earth wants to be in relationship with us. These early disciples received the same call every Jesus follower hears: "Go make disciples of every nation." The mission is clear. Every woman, man, and child deserves to know they are loved, valued, and in need of a Savior. "The harvest is plentiful but the workers are few" (Matt. 9:37). We all are called to pray that the loving God of the universe will send workers out on his mission. As we pray, we should raise our hands and say, "God, choose me. Send me. Help me to be faithful to your mission."

Jesus Loved People

We were at a national evangelism conference in the Chicago area, and I (Kevin) was giving an evangelism presentation with a dear friend and partner in the gospel, Mark Mittelberg. At the end of our talk, people were invited to come to a microphone and ask questions. A man got up and presented his quandary. "I have a neighbor I don't really get along with or like. I know I am supposed to evangelize him, but we have little in common, and I don't enjoy being around him. What should I do?"

In retrospect, my response was a bit harsh, but I felt it needed to be said. "Stay away from him." I continued, "Pray that God will raise up someone else to share Jesus with him. Then pray for love to grow in your heart. If you reach out to him as a project or religious duty, he will feel it, smell it, know it. Until you have love for him, it is best to leave outreach to someone else." You might agree or disagree with my words to this man. But either way, when we seek to share the good news and love of Jesus with people, it is always helpful if we really love them. That was Jesus' starting point in every human encounter.

Jesus loved all sorts of people. Jesus was, and is, the sinless Lamb of God. His attributes are identical to those of the Father and the Holy Spirit. Jesus is holy, holy, holy, Lord God Almighty. Yet he loved and took delight in ordinary people. There was a family that lived in the city of Bethany: Mary, Martha, and their brother, Lazarus. When Jesus was told that Lazarus was sick, the words were, "The one you love is sick" (John 11:3). And the Scriptures tell us that Jesus had great love in his heart for Mary, Martha, and Lazarus (John 11:5).

Jesus wept over people he loved (John 11:35–36). John was called "the disciple whom Jesus loved" (John 21:20). As Jesus sat at the Last Supper with his followers, we are told that he loved them to the end (John 13:1). In a broad and sweeping declaration, Jesus himself said, "Greater love has no one than this: to lay down one's life for one's friends" (John 15:13). Then Jesus did exactly that—for you and for me! Jesus' love was deep and wide and transcended every human barrier.

Jesus loved the "unlovable." In every time and culture, there are people who seem to be hard to love. Jesus made it a point to reach out to such people. One of his closest friends and trusted ministry partners was a tax collector. That kind of person was hated, suspected, and distrusted by the people of that day. Yet Jesus loved Matthew and called him to follow him (Matt. 9:9–13). The sinless Lord spent time with tax collectors, prostitutes, and sinners (Matt. 11:19; Mark 2:15–16; Luke 15:1–7), and the religious professionals of the day were upset that these people loved Jesus and he loved them back.

The Savior called on his followers to love their enemies (Matt. 5:44). Broken women felt free to draw near to Jesus and express their love, and he welcomed them (Luke 7:36–38). Zacchaeus, the "wee little man" sung about in a children's song, was an "unlovable" whom Jesus embraced with grace and dignity. The four gospels overflow with accounts of Jesus' love for those whom most religious and well-mannered people avoided.

Jesus loved the unprotected and vulnerable. In the ancient world, there were no social-service programs or safety nets for those who were hurting and in need. Certain groups of people were vulnerable and in danger of being forgotten. Widows (and women in general), orphans, children, people with sicknesses (like leprosy), and other groups were in constant danger and often survived on the outskirts of society. Jesus was always looking out for these people, his heart broke for them, and he clearly loved them. Jesus trained his eye on the fringes of society to see whether there were forgotten and outcast people who needed a touch of his love. If we were to do a study of Jesus' loving care for these people, it could warrant an entire book. As you read through the Gospels, take special note of Jesus' attention to the marginalized and forgotten. Let his example open your eyes and heart to these people today, and seek to love them as Jesus does.

Real Life and Real Relationships

Since Jesus came as one of us and walked among us, his relational life and the community he shared with people were just as real as ours. We can learn from watching Jesus' commitment to consistent community.

Jesus had varied relational connections. As we study the life of Jesus, we see that our Savior related to people in a wide spectrum of settings and groups. He had a love for the crowds and spent a lot of time teaching, sharing meals, and enjoying being with very large groups of people (Matt. 12:15, 46; 13:34). He also had an extensive network of more than seventy followers whom he invested in and sent on mission (Luke 10:1–4). These were people he spent time with and poured into. It is also clear in the Scriptures that he was particularly close to a family of siblings, Lazarus, Mary, and Martha. This family offered hospitality to Jesus and had a special relationship with him.

As the concentric relational circles move closer to Jesus, we find the twelve disciples (Mark 3:13–19). This is the relational group that people most identify with the Savior. These men walked with Jesus, received intense mentoring, watched his ministry up close, and experienced his friendship personally. Jesus sent them to preach his message, battle spiritual forces, and minister in his name. They were the ones gathered with Jesus at the Last Supper as the Lord washed their feet, broke the bread, poured out the cup, and called them to radical service (John 13:1–17).

Within this group of friends and ministry partners was an even smaller company of disciples. Peter, James, and John received more intense training and were invited into some of the most significant and intimate moments of Jesus' life. It was these three that the Savior brought with him to the Mount of Transfiguration when Moses and Elijah appeared and Yahweh spoke the words, "This is my Son, whom I love; with him I am well pleased. Listen to him!" (Matt. 17:5). When Jesus went to raise a young girl from the dead, he asked the three to join him (Mark 5:37–40). In his moment of great spiritual agony preparing to carry the cross for our sins, it was Peter, James, and John whom Jesus took with him to the garden of Gethsemane (Matt. 26:36–46). The Lord wanted his closest friends to be with him and to pray.

When we look at the life of our Savior, we do not see a disconnected and dispassionate spiritual being floating an inch off the ground. We encounter one who was fully human, yet without sin, who loved people and made community a central part of his life.

Broken relationships broke the heart of Jesus. Not only did our Lord delight in friendships, he mourned when people were divided and relationships were fractured. In the Sermon on the Mount, Jesus made it clear that the healing of a broken relationship is cause to walk out of a worship service for the purpose of seeking reconciliation (Matt. 5:23–24). When we have been wronged by a sister or a brother, it is such a big deal to Jesus that he gave us a multistep process to seek restoration (Matt. 18:15–17). When the poison of unforgiveness devastates community and family love, we are to forgive as God in Christ forgave us and extend heavenly grace as many times as seventy times seven (Matt. 18:21–22). Our Lord taught his followers to guard their words and never call someone a fool or an "empty-headed one." One of the reasons Jesus came into our world was to break down barriers based on race and human differences and unite people as one family (Eph. 2:11–18). We are to be careful when tempted to become judge, jury, and executioner of those who wrong us (Matt. 7:1–2). Again and again, Jesus calls us to walk in unity, and he wanted it so deeply that he prayed for it (John 17:11).

Jesus felt the knife thrust of abandonment and broken relationships. Our Lord was so human that he felt what we feel, physically, emotionally, spiritually, in every way. Jesus allowed himself to get so close to people that their betrayal hurt. When Judas, one of his twelve closest friends, sold him out for some precious metal, Jesus felt the cut (Matt. 26:14–16). When Peter denied him publicly and repeatedly, the Lord was right there listening and watching it all unfold (Luke 22:54–62). He must have felt those gut punches. In a moment of great need, while he was being arrested, everyone deserted him and ran away (Mark 14:50). We can't pretend this did not hurt our Savior. The one whose heart broke when he saw shattered relationships must have felt the pain of abandonment, betrayal, and denial.

The gracious risen Lord called his followers back to him. Jesus calls followers, and when they fall short and deny him, doubt him, and disappear, he calls them back to himself. When Peter denied Jesus, he thought the dream was over and his invitation to follow and serve the Lord was revoked. When the risen Lord came looking for Peter, he found him out fishing—back to life and work as it was before Jesus had first met him on the shore of the Sea of Galilee three years earlier. Jesus called him back (John 21:15–19) and gave him freedom to affirm his devotion again and again and again. Then he said these words: "You must follow me" (John 21:22). Imagine the life-giving freedom and hope those words brought. Jesus was telling Peter, "We are still friends. You can still follow me. You still have a mission—my mission. I know what you have done, but our relationship can endure even this. Keep following me, and let's move forward."

Jesus says the same to us when we stumble and fall. Community means so much to Jesus that he calls us to walk with him and calls us back every time we wander away.

CHAPTER 20

Better Together: Why We > Me

I (Sherry) have never known life outside the community of God's family. I was not a pastor's kid, but you could say I grew up in the church. We were in church every Sunday morning for worship and then Sunday school, and in the evening, our whole family was back at church for another time of worship and the second sermon of the day. On Wednesday evening, we were with the family of God for the midweek classes and fellowship. There were also youth groups and special events. The community of Christ's people was the air we breathed, and I loved it.

There were many Sundays when my family was one of the last to leave because they were waiting for me. I loved talking with the people at my church. I felt the strength and goodness of being part of God's family. From my youngest days, I had a conviction that Christians belong to each other and are stronger, healthier, and better together.

We Were Made for Community

Years later I went to a great Christian college and then seminary. In my Bible and theology courses, I learned the theological underpinnings of why as God's people we are stronger as a group than we are by ourselves.

The imago Dei. God exists in eternal, perfect community in the Godhead. Christians are monotheists, meaning that we believe there is one God and only one. Yet this God does not exist in isolation. God exists as three eternal persons, Father, Son, and Holy Spirit. One in being, existing in perfect unity as three persons— God is perfect community.

When we read of God's creation of humankind, it should not surprise us that we are also made for community. "Then God said, 'Let us make mankind in our image, in our likeness, so that they may rule over the fish in the sea and the birds in the sky, over the livestock and all the wild animals, and over all the creatures that move along the ground.' So God created mankind in his own image, in the image of God he created them; male and female he created them. God blessed them and said to them, 'Be fruitful and increase in number'" (Gen. 1:26–28).

In this short passage, we read three times that God made us in his image. Part of that image (the *imago Dei*) is our communal nature. Men and women, together, reflect the image of God in community with one another.

Notice God's first command right after creating people. It is a community directive to make more people (Gen. 1:28)! Adam and Eve were called to create. In intimate communion with each other (the relationship of marriage), they were to make a growing community for the glory of God.

We > me. All through the Scriptures, we learn that God accomplishes more for his glory through his people together than if they are disconnected. When the apostle Paul started churches all over the ancient world, he taught the early Christians that their mission and calling would be fulfilled only if they functioned like a body (Rom. 12:3–8; 1 Cor. 12:12–31). Every person is needed and valuable. No one can say, "I don't matter," or, "You are not needed."

The connection between God's people is greater than most of us realize. In the climax of Paul's teaching on the church, Paul writes, "If one part suffers, every part suffers with it; if one part is honored, every part rejoices with it" (1 Cor. 12:26). Like a physical body with a central nervous system that ties every part together, members of God's family are connected to one another. It is a beautiful spiritual reality.

The Great Commandment. When the religious leaders of Jesus' day tried to trap Jesus and paint him into a theological corner, they asked him, "What is the most important commandment?" Of all the things Jesus could have said, and there were a lot of commands to choose from, he focused on one idea. If we distill it to one word, it would be *community.* Jesus reminded them of the commands to love God and love people. What matters most is relationships, both vertical and horizontal (Mark 12:29–31). The Great Commandment is all about living in a life-giving community with our Creator and his created ones.

Why Is Community So Complex?

If God exists in perfect eternal community and we are called to seek healthy relationships above all else, why is it so difficult? If consistent community is one of the primary indicators we are walking closely with Jesus, why is it so complex?

We cannot ignore the sobering reality of sin. We are all sinners. Every human being is tainted by their own brokenness. In Jesus we find grace, and by his Spirit we can learn to love and forgive, but it is a lifelong battle. On this side of eternity, every person, including followers of Jesus, needs to recognize their potential for evil and fight against it.

I (Kevin) have been a pastor for more than three decades. I have lots of friends who serve the church. And I have not met a single church leader who has not been attacked and hurt by one or more of their church members during their years of ministry. Marshall Shelley wrote a book many years ago titled *Well-Intentioned Dragons: Ministering to Problem People in Your Church*. To this day, it is one of the best ministry books I have ever read. It addresses the reality that some people think they are helping, but they end up doing great damage to their pastors or other church leaders and church members.

I believe Shelley could have written a companion book titled *Well-Intentioned Leaders: Ministering to Problem Pastors in Your Church*. You see, every pastor I know would also admit that they have made poor choices, gotten angry, and hurt people in their congregation. The sobering reality is that we are all sinners being transformed by God's grace. We are growing in sanctification, but we have not arrived yet. If we are not careful, we cut others with our sharp edges. When we do life with other people (even in the church), there is always a danger of getting hurt. If we are looking to glide through life with no pain, we will have to avoid all human contact, even contact in the church.

We live in an isolating culture. People used to maintain uninterrupted eye contact while having conversations. Families and friends would go out for dinner and interact exclusively with the people at their table. Through an entire meal, the only interruption was when the server came to get the order. Years ago, living rooms were arranged so that all the furniture was in a square or circle so that all the people were facing each other. All of this has been disrupted.

Technology has created massive isolation. During most conversations, our attention is intermittently drawn toward screens on devices we carry in our pockets or wear on our wrists. Eye contact is broken, and conversations are fragmented. Dinners out are invaded by tweets, emails, calls, and advertisements buzzing and beeping. Living rooms are arranged with the furniture oriented toward a large monitor designed to pipe in entertainment. We might occupy the same space in a living room, but we are often focused on media and not human connection.

There is great value to much of the technology we have, but community building is not one of them. Life-to-life, eye-to-eye, and heart-to-heart connection can be severed as we find ourselves slaves of the tools that should serve us. We have more "connections," but less intimacy. We have virtual friends, but few people who will pick us up at the airport at midnight. Isolation is an enemy of community, and the media culture that screams for our attention leads to loneliness, even when we are not alone.

We have all felt the pain of broken community. Past pain causes a reflexive response of pulling away. Only a fool touches a scalding hot pan and then reaches out and grabs it again. In the same way, when we have felt the pain of betrayal and broken community, it is natural to distance ourselves from others. When that pain comes from people who bear the name of Jesus and who call themselves our church family, it is easy to reflexively remove ourselves from that community.

Satan hates consistent and life-giving community. To make matters worse, Satan knows the world-changing power of Christian community. He hates healthy churches, loving small groups, welcoming youth ministries, and dynamic bodies of believers. The powers of hell rage against the ministry and community life of a church. The liar and Father of Lies does all he can to keep us from being connected, supportive, caring, and in love with the family of God in our churches.

Devoting Ourselves to Consistent Community

God Almighty loves his church, the bride, the family, the body of the Lord Jesus Christ. Knowing this, and being profoundly aware of the complexity of building healthy congregations, disciples of Jesus need to commit to doing all we can to grow community in the family of believers. This can happen in formal church settings and in the rhythm of daily life.

The power of the table. Jesus knew the intimacy and glory of a good meal shared with others. Near the beginning of his ministry, at the advent of Jesus' first public miracle, the Lord of Glory was at a party (John 2:1–11). This wedding reception created a place for the sharing of life, celebration, and the enjoyment of good wine and good friends. Near the end of his life, Jesus broke bread and poured out the cup with his closest friends as they shared the Passover meal (Matt. 26:17–30). At the table, Jesus taught about servanthood, the future, and the meaning of his sacrifice. After his resurrection, Jesus prepared a meal along the lakeside and conversed with some of his followers. This outdoor meal was an opportunity for restoration and preparation for the future (John 21:9–24).

In a busy and hectic world, Christians need to rediscover the power of lingering over a meal with brothers and sisters in faith. Share life by praying for each other, telling stories, laughing and crying together. Table fellowship creates a place to move from casual chatting to deep conversation. If disciples of Jesus are to live as he did, we need to spend more time around tables sharing food and life.[29]

The joy of a good walk. Jesus also engaged in life-giving community with others as they walked together. Do a study sometime about all that happened while Jesus was walking. It is astounding! At the start of Jesus' public ministry, he called followers as he was walking along the Sea of Galilee (Matt. 4:18–22). The first thing they did was to begin walking with him. After his resurrection, Jesus joined a couple of men who were taking a walk and having a talk. The resurrected Lord of Glory, who had just destroyed the power of hell, won the victory over Satan, and bought our salvation with his life, went for a stroll and had a rich conversation (Luke 24:13–35).

Disciples need to ask this life-changing question more often than we do: "Can we take a walk?" As we do, God shows up.

Preferably we will do this with our phones silenced, left behind, or turned off. (Yes, that is allowed.) One of the best places to have spiritual conversations is anywhere we can take a walk. We can do this with younger believers as we help them grow in faith. We can also do this with people who have graciously taken our hand and are helping us grow to love Jesus more.

The life-giving gift of blessing. Words of kindness and encouragement build community. Thoughtless words can burn like fire. As followers of Jesus, we can speak grace, extend forgiveness, and build people up with kindness spoken in the name of our Lord.

People, even deeply broken people, were drawn to the Savior. One reason is that his words spoke life and hope. When a sinful woman was caught in the act of adultery and anticipated judgment in the form of words, stares, and stones, Jesus spoke life. "Neither do I condemn you. . . . Go now and leave your life of sin" (John 8:11). When a hated tax collector responded to the grace of Jesus, our Savior declared, "Today salvation has come to this house" (Luke 19:9). Imagine the healing these words brought to his soul. When a lifelong criminal used one of his last gasps for breath to ask Jesus to remember him, our crucified Lord declared, "Today you will be with me in paradise" (Luke 23:43). When Peter believed he had fallen from grace and was no longer qualified to be a disciple, the risen Lord told him, "You must follow me" (John 21:22).

We who follow Jesus must master the art of blessing. Every chance we have, we can speak words that uplift and heal. In a world that tears down, we can build up. Consistent community is not just about being together, it is about how we relate to each other. Words have power! A commitment to bless others with what we say unleashes the grace and presence of Jesus.

The beauty of everyone. In heaven, we will all be together. Let this biblical picture fill your mind and heart: "After this I looked, and there before me was a great multitude that no one could count, from every nation, tribe, people and language, standing before the throne and before the Lamb. They were wearing white robes and were holding palm branches in their hands. And they cried out in a loud voice: 'Salvation belongs to our God, who sits on the throne, and to the Lamb'" (Rev. 7:9–10).

Our eternity will be a staggeringly beautiful gathering of our brothers and sisters from every people group in the world. We need to seek and embrace this picture of God's family in our lives and churches today. As we do, the world will look at the church and see the kind of loving and harmonious diversity that so many say they want, but so few seem to be able to find. Christians should see the beauty of everyone because we look through the eyes of Jesus. Let's join our hearts and lives in this holy pursuit before we go to heaven.

The glory of tenacious unity. Our world is polarized, embattled, and embittered. Families are torn apart, and people with differing points of view have a hard time talking to, listening to, and understanding each other. Racial tensions are increasing, political disagreements are growing, and anger is simmering as the media stokes the fire every chance it gets.

The church of Jesus should be an example of unity and community, even when we see things with differing points of view. We can still love each other. Of all the people in the world, the group that should be an example of tenacious unity, even when we see things differently, is the body of Jesus. When the world looks at Christians, it should see people from every tribe, nation, and people group who love each other like family, because that is what we are. The world should see a body of people who are committed to loving each other and walking in unity no matter what cultural battles are raging.

This unity transcends our circle of Christian friends and the congregations where we worship and serve. Jesus-honoring unity calls us to love brothers and sisters in other Christian fellowships around our communities, nations, and world. We honor Jesus and send a message to the world when we pray for, serve with, and love other congregations of Jesus followers.

The womb of Christian maturity. The community of God's people is where we grow up in faith. Maturity is birthed in fellowship with other believers who love Jesus and seek to walk in his footsteps. Church services, small groups of believers, loving Christian families, Jesus-centered friendships, and discipling relationships are all incubators that God uses to help us grow in faith.

No matter what our temperament or perceived need to be around other people, we were made for community. When we come to faith in Jesus, we hear his call to love and be loved in the family of God. New believers and longtime followers of Jesus all need to have someone take their hand and help them forward in faith. We also need to do the same for someone who is behind us on this glorious journey of following Jesus. This can happen only when we engage in consistent community with God's family.

4 Generation Challenge (2-2-2)

Through the highs and lows of my life, God has surrounded me (Sherry) with godly women who have become a community of love and grace. These are people I can be myself with and know that they will still love me. I am blessed to have several godly women who have taken my hand and are helping me experience the community life of the body of Christ. They know me, love me, and model Christian community in a way that helps me grow as a disciple. In my life, they are my generation 1.

I am the second-generation disciple influenced by these godly women. I am responsible to live in community in the church and with believers everywhere. I am called by my Lord to tend to my engagement in Christian community and make sure I do not pull away because of the multitude of challenges inherent in church life. Only I can partner with the Holy Spirit to discern where my gifts and energies can be used to build healthy community.

It would be easy to stop there and say, "I have people who help me grow in community, and I am doing my part to engage in the life of God's family. That's enough!" But as you know by now, that is not the whole story. I am called by the Lord to reach back and take the hand of someone who also needs to grow in consistent community.

One of those people whom both Kevin and I were able to invest in was a woman named Kata. She came to our church while living on the streets in a motor home. For her first year at Shoreline, we helped her walk toward Jesus. We prayed with her, listened to her stories, and shared the message of God's love and grace again and again. We loved her and wanted her to know she was welcome at our church. During this time, she told us she was not an atheist but was still dabbling in Buddhism, Taoism, Judaism, and mysticism. She was curious about the Christian faith and intrigued by Jesus, and though Kata was not a Christian, she was open to the gospel. On a couple of occasions, she talked about becoming a Christian, but her desire really was to add Jesus to her growing array of religious systems and figures.

A number of other women in our church also took Kata's hand and walked with her toward Jesus. She became a part of our church and was engaged in all sorts of ministries and fellowship opportunities. She began to attend everything she could. She was not a believer in Jesus, but she was a part of the church family with dozens of people taking her hand and walking with her. It was beautiful!

Eventually, she came to the point where she was ready to receive Jesus and pledge her allegiance to him alone as her Lord. After Kata accepted the lavish love of the Savior, she continued in the community of our church. A number of women helped her forward in spiritual growth. Her love for worship and her joy over God's goodness were contagious.

Eventually, she rented a room in a home, got a good job, and through the years reached out to many people in our community whom others could not reach. She has taken their hands and helped others journey toward Jesus. One Sunday after a rainy week, Kata told us that she had gone to Home Depot and bought a number of tarps and set up tent areas for some of her friends who were still living on the streets. She said, "I have so much, and I just love to help people who don't have all that I do!" She was taking their hands and slowly walking with them toward Jesus, just like I and a few other women at Shoreline had done with her.

Do you get the picture? Four generations of hands and hearts locked together growing in consistent community. This is organic discipleship.

CHAPTER 21

The World Will Know We Are Christians by the Way We Love One Another . . . and Them!

Some stories lock themselves in your mind and stay with you forever. This is one of them. It was shared with us by our dear friend Nabeel Qureshi as he spoke about how Christians can help Muslims learn to understand Jesus and the faith of his followers. It is a story that broke our hearts, an account of community missed.

A young Muslim man moved to the United States to study. He arrived with only two suitcases. In one were his clothes and the essential items he needed for his years of study in this new and intriguing place. In the second was a collection of gifts from his homeland. He brought many thoughtful items that spoke of his heritage, culture, and home.

Why did he use half the space he had to bring these items? They were gifts for all the people who would invite him into their homes and share their lives with him. Each one was personally chosen and had its own story. These items would be a way to thank and honor people for opening their homes and hearts to a young man who came from a world away. They would spark conversation while sharing a meal together. In his culture, bringing a gift when coming into a home for the first time was a common practice. He was excited to see who would receive each of the treasures he had brought.

A few years later, this same man, now a little less young and a little more jaded, packed up to head back to his homeland. Once again, he had two suitcases. One held his clothes. And the other was filled with the same gifts he had brought with him years before. Not one single gift had been given, because no one had invited him into their home. The community his heart longed for was never realized. Friendships were never forged, and the gifts remained ungiven.

How many Christians did this young man meet during his years in the States? Dozens? Hundreds? How deeply did he long for community? What might have happened if followers of Jesus had invited him into their homes and hearts?

Every person we meet hungers for community. It is a universal desire. If we learn from Jesus' example and embrace consistent community, this can become a conduit for the gospel in powerful and life-changing ways.

People Are Drawn to Christians Engaged in Consistent Community

Jesus was magnetic! Broken people called on his name. Powerful leaders sought him out. Marginalized people felt safe with him. The masses were drawn to his teaching and ministry. Jesus never tried to drum up crowds or pressure people to come near him. He simply loved people and they sensed it. They loved him too. Multitudes gathered. People came near the Savior.

Christians are filled with the Spirit of God. We are followers of the Savior. The love of our heavenly Father is alive in our hearts. If we lift up Jesus and follow him, he will draw people to himself, toward his disciples, near to us.

As his followers, we can make room to establish community with friends, family, and new acquaintances who are not yet believers in Jesus. We can open our hearts, schedules, and homes and invite people in. There are folks we cross paths with on a regular basis who are much like the young Muslim man who desired to find the gift of community and give a gift in return. They are waiting for someone to say, "Would you like to come over?" "Could I make dinner for you?" "Let's hang out and get to know each other." The world wants what Christians have—consistent and loving community. The question is, will we offer it?

Too often fear keeps us at arm's length, busyness prevails, and we miss divine appointments to extend community. As Christians, we have this amazing gift. Let's share it with others. If people are going to see Jesus, they need to get close to those who know the Lord and shine his light. Availability and attentiveness are keys to community. We need to slow down and notice the people God places in our lives. We can't be so occupied serving the church or hanging out with other Christians that we miss the opportunity to spend meaningful time with people who are far from Jesus.

Homes Filled with Jesus' Presence Shine His Light

Christian homes can be havens in our broken world. By building a loving community right where we live, we can show others the hope of Jesus. We do not have to be perfect—no family is. What we can do is model love, respect, and care within a family. When Jesus is present, people are drawn in. Imagine homes in every neighborhood where grace, love, and forgiveness are clear to see. People will notice and Jesus will be revealed. This is the desire of God's heart.

Years ago, we wrote a book titled *Organic Outreach for Families: Turning Your Home into a Lighthouse*. The idea is that every home where Jesus is welcome and rules as Lord can be a beacon of light in a dark world. Every Christian marriage and family that is seeking to live and love like Jesus can have massive impact for the gospel. When a loving community exists in a home and family, others in that neighborhood will see it and be drawn toward the community their hearts long for.

Churches That Welcome People into Community Honor God

I (Kevin) had the privilege of training church leaders in El Salvador. Our focus was on how to grow churches that love the lost and share the gospel in winsome and welcoming ways. During the event, I talked about how we should embrace people right where they are and how to develop a "come as you are" culture in the church. I offered a few examples and watched the faces of the leaders to get a sense of how well they were connecting with the concept. I had a team of three translators who would tag team in and out every thirty minutes. I would share a thought and then watch the faces of the church leaders as one of the translators communicated what I had just said.

At a specific moment, I knew I had hit a nerve. I said, "If a woman walks into your church and she is wearing jeans and a T-shirt, you should welcome her with joy and embrace her with love." The weekend before, I had noticed that everyone in the church services was dressed formally. I could see by the expressions on some faces that this was a questionable idea. I even saw some scowls of disagreement.

During the break, a few of the women leaders came up to me. One of them said, "If a woman came to our church and she was not dressed appropriately, we would ask her to leave." I waited. Another one of the women asked, with tears forming in her eyes, "That is wrong, isn't it?" They clearly were struggling. In El Salvador, there were strong cultural norms about how a person should look and dress when they come into the house of the Lord. I was not trying to upset their mores and church practices, but wanted to help them get to the heart of God for lost people.

This encounter led to a great conversation about how non-believers should be treated on their way to Jesus. Can we welcome them just as they are? What would Jesus do in this situation? Did he ever push someone away because of how they dressed or looked? Can the church be a place of community for those who are still deep in sin, far from God, or simply unaware of how we church people do things?[30]

Imagine what could happen if every follower of Jesus modeled loving community and embraced people who have not yet met Jesus as Savior. Next, imagine if every home where believers dwell sought to reflect the consistent and grace-filled community Jesus came to offer. Finally, let yourself dream about what could happen if every Christian church committed to welcoming people into their fellowship, community life, and hearts long before they placed faith in the Savior.

The Power and Witness of Consistent Community

How can community in our lives, homes, and churches draw people to Jesus and open the door for the gospel? When we invite spiritual seekers into our lives, they can see Jesus at work. The lies of the enemy are stripped away, and they can experience the love, grace, and presence of God firsthand.

In community, people will encounter love in action. It is hard to see love with a telescope. It is best observed up close and personal. When we invite lost people into community, they can see how Christians love one another, and this sends a powerful message. Jesus put it this way: "A new command I give you: Love one another. As I have loved you, so you must love one another. By this everyone will know that you are my disciples, if you love one another" (John 13:34–35).

Ask yourself, "If I invite a nonbelieving friend into my life, my home, or my church, will they be amazed by the love they see between Christians?" This is one of the most important aspects of our witness to the world. We are called to love the believers God places in our lives. Make time to express your affection to those who live in your home. Be a church that overflows with kindness and care for one another. Love believers who are part of other Christian fellowships in your town and talk about what they mean to you. They are family. The world needs to see how we love one another. Then they will know we are Christians.

In community, people will see forgiveness at work. One of the most countercultural things a Christian can do is to extend forgiveness. When we invite spiritual seekers into community, they get a front-row seat to the lives of the forgiven and forgiving. The apostle Paul called Jesus' people to a lifestyle of grace and graciousness. "Be kind and compassionate to one another, forgiving each other, just as in Christ God forgave you" (Eph. 4:32). When nonbelievers engage in a community of people who forgive freely and consistently, they see the presence and power of Jesus at work.

Ask yourself, "Am I committed to forgiveness at such a deep level that it shows? Or am I quick to judge and slow to let go of hurts?" Christians are a community of radically and divinely forgiven people. We are washed, loved, and cleansed! Our reflexive response should be grace and forgiveness. If it is not, we need to spend some time at the foot of the cross, looking into the face of our Savior, who cried out, "Father, forgive them, for they do not know what they are doing" (Luke 23:34). Create a community of forgiveness, and invite people in to see what Jesus offers.

In community, people will see unity in diversity. It is easy to look at our world and feel that polarization and division are the worst they have ever been. If we could go back to the first century, when Jesus walked on this planet, we would find a time when human conflict was deep and demonic on many levels. The chasm between Jews and gentiles was greater than the Grand Canyon. Slaves and free people lived in different worlds. Men and women felt the gender rift growing wider and wider. Into this conflicted situation,

Jesus came to destroy "the barrier, the dividing wall of hostility" (Eph. 2:14). Inspired by the Holy Spirit of peace, the apostle Paul wrote these words: "So in Christ Jesus you are all children of God through faith, for all of you who were baptized into Christ have clothed yourselves with Christ. There is neither Jew nor Gentile, neither slave nor free, nor is there male and female, for you are all one in Christ Jesus" (Gal. 3:26–28).

Three of the biggest divisions in the ancient world, as referenced in this passage, were torn down and removed by Jesus. Of all the places in the world, the church and Christian community should be a model of people from every walk of life living in unity. Our churches should look like our community, in all of its diverse beauty.

Look at your life, your home, and your church. What can you do to create unity in the midst of a conflicted world? How can you partner with Jesus to tear down walls? How can you make sure that everyone knows they are welcome, because they are? What words can you speak? Who can you love? Where do you need to repent? When we seek to walk in unity, even with deep differences, we create an atmosphere where the gospel comes alive and people see the presence of the Savior.

In community, people will see collaborative service. Where will you see corporate CEOs helping set up chairs or teaching children's classes for free? In the church! Where can you find groups of people working together to accomplish a common cause in a city or town? Any place churches have learned to serve together in the name of Jesus. Some years ago, a group of Christian churches from around Monterey County decided to unite in serving the community. They established a movement called Love Our Central Coast.

At different times in the course of the year, these congregations work together on behalf of public schools, government agencies, the parks department, businesses, and anyone who can use a little help. These followers of Jesus not only work together but partner with people in the community to love and serve those in need.

Picture a park cleanup crew made up of firefighters, kids from the community who play at that park, curious teens who wander over to see what's up, and a bunch of Jesus followers from a variety of churches in the community. Together they sift every square foot of sand and remove pound after pound of broken glass, sharp metal objects, and garbage of every sort. Swings, slides, and play equipment receive fresh coats of paint. Broken benches are repaired. Friendships are forged. Laughter and conversation erupt as people work together. Questions are asked by those who live in that community. "Why are all of you here cleaning up our park?" "Are you getting paid for this?" "Where are all of you from?" Each question is a conduit for stories of God's love, presence, and grace.

In community, people will see the presence and power of the Holy Spirit. Most nonbelievers have no idea that God is present and actually working in people's lives. When we invite them into community, we can share about what God is doing. Our stories of testimony reveal the actions of the Holy Spirit in the lives of ordinary people. Imagine an atheist or agnostic person listening to stories of lives, families, and marriages that have been healed by a touch of the Spirit. How will they respond when Christians talk about answered prayer? Christians have stories to tell about receiving direction, hope in hard times, meaning in the emptiness of life, and purpose that gets them out of bed every morning. We can't share these accounts of God's work from far away. We need to be close, in community.[31]

Lost people long for more. They are made for community, and we have what their hearts long for. Jesus calls us to live in consistent community and invite people to join us. It can be personal friendships, an invitation into our homes, or connections in the life of the church. When spiritually curious people are wrapped into the community of God's people, they can see, hear, and experience the presence of the resurrected Lord of Glory.

PART 7

Organic Outreach

Love as I Have Loved You

The first one to reach out is always God. He so loved the world that he gave his only Son. When Jesus walked on this earth, he extended grace to every person he met. We who follow Jesus are to love people as he does. Every disciple carries the best news in human history. Our calling is to share the love and gospel of Jesus freely, in the power of the Spirit. As we partner with the Savior, he draws people to himself, and he alone receives the glory.

CHAPTER 22

The Evangelist of All Evangelists

Jesus Had a Clear Mission

Many organizations can be identified by a few words or a short sentence. Pictures come to mind when you hear a slogan or saying. "Just Do It!" "The Happiest Place on Earth." "Semper Fi." "Think Different." "The Quicker Picker Upper." "I'm Lovin' It." "It's Finger Lickin' Good!" "Seek and Save the Lost." How many of these can you identify? Here is a quick answer key: Nike, Disney, US Marine Corps, Apple, Bounty, McDonald's, KFC. But can you identify the final example? It's not a corporation or a modern nonprofit. It's the mission statement of Jesus Christ. Let's see where this phrase originated.

After Jesus entered the home and life of the tax collector Zacchaeus, this extortionist was transformed. His heart and actions changed as he came under the lordship of Jesus. In response, our Savior declared these words: "Today salvation has come to this house" (Luke 19:9). Then Jesus made a powerful declaration about himself. Often, when our Lord referred to himself, he used the title the Son of Man. In this case, Jesus was definitive when he said, "The Son of Man came to seek and to save the lost" (Luke 19:10).

This was the mission of our Lord. Everything else seemed to

connect to this calling and passion. From the beginning, when Adam and Eve rebelled and were enslaved to their sin, the Son of God was committed to save broken and sin-sick humanity. This is why the Word took on flesh and walked among us (John 1:14). The angelic messengers knew this and declared that Jesus' mission was to be our Savior (Luke 2:8–12). To the ancient prophets and to those who witnessed the baby lying in the manger, it was clear that the one who came was on a mission to save the lost. After a lifetime of waiting, Simeon went to the temple courtyard at the exact time Joseph and Mary arrived with their son. Simeon held the baby Jesus in his arms and declared these words:

> "Sovereign Lord, as you have promised,
>> you may now dismiss your servant in peace.
> For my eyes have seen your salvation,
>> which you have prepared in the sight of all
>>> nations:
> a light for revelation to the Gentiles,
>> and the glory of your people Israel."
>
> —Luke 2:29–32

Who Was This Jesus?

All through the Gospels, Jesus declared who he was. Others added their voices and became a chorus of witnesses proclaiming that the Savior King had come. Many of the names and descriptions clarified Jesus' mission and plan for the world. We who call ourselves disciples need to know exactly who he was. When we do, we have clarity on who we serve and how he wants us to live.

The Messiah. Many people in the first century were waiting for the arrival of the Messiah, the one who would deliver them. The people longed for the Anointed One, their Savior, to come, but some were anticipating a political and military conqueror. Others thought he would bring religious freedom. No one realized the glory, power, and absolute victory that Jesus, the Messiah, would win through his life, death, and resurrection.

In the middle of Jesus' theological conversation with a Samaritan woman, recorded in the Gospel of John, the woman touched on this theme. She explained to Jesus (imagine the irony) that she was confident that the Messiah would come one day. She told him that the Messiah would clear up all misunderstandings. Jesus responded with unflinching clarity, "I, the one speaking to you—I am he" (John 4:26). Our Lord could not have been any clearer. Jesus is the Messiah—our Messiah—and salvation has come. Deliverance is here.

The Bread of Heaven. In the Old Testament, God gave manna, bread from heaven, to sustain his people and reveal his glory, provision, and love (Exodus 16). When Jesus spoke to his followers, he told them that he was heavenly bread and that partaking of him would lead to eternal life (John 6:48–58). With boldness and precision, Jesus declared that those who feast on him will live forever.

The Living Water. We all know that food and water are essential for life. Cut off the supply of either long enough and even the strongest of people grows weak and eventually dies. Jesus stood up on the last day of a festival in Jerusalem and lifted his voice: "Let anyone who is thirsty come to me and drink" (John 7:37). He promised not only that he would satisfy their thirst but that they would be so saturated they would overflow with rivers of living water. What was Jesus saying? In a desert land where water was essential to stay alive, he was pointing to himself as the source of so much refreshment and life that they would have more than enough.

The Light of the World. In a world of darkness, we have a light. His name is Jesus. We do not have to live in fear. We can tell others that there is light that can illuminate their path. In John's Gospel, we see a direct connection between receiving the light of Jesus, believing in his name, and becoming part of God's family (John 1:12–13). We who walk in his light also shine that light wherever we go.

The Lamb of God. When John the Baptist saw Jesus, his response was, "Look, the Lamb of God" (John 1:29). But he did not stop there. John added, "Who takes away the sin of the world." The people who heard these words would have pictured exactly what John meant. In our minds today, we imagine a cute and fluffy lamb, maybe the kind you would see in a children's Bible book prancing through a lovely meadow. If you do a Google image search for "Passover lamb," you'll find that most of the pictures are tame and sanitized.

But what would have come to the mind of the average person on the street in the days of Jesus and John the Baptist? Probably a memory of a Passover lamb slaughtered. They would have thought of the blood of a young lamb killed as a reminder of God's protection and salvation from slavery in Egypt. They would have recognized that John was pointing at Jesus and saying, "This one will die for our sins, as a sacrifice for us."

The Good Shepherd. It might seem strange when we hear that John the Baptist called Jesus the Lamb of God, and then later, Jesus called himself the Good Shepherd. At first glance, it might seem confusing: Is Jesus a shepherd or a sheep? The answer is, both! Both of these are beautiful word pictures given to help our limited minds comprehend the vastness of his glory. Not only did Jesus die like a sacrificial lamb, he also protects like a loving shepherd.

Jesus said, "I am the good shepherd. The good shepherd lays down his life for the sheep" (John 10:11). It is a picture of love and an image of diligent protection. It's a vision of pastoral care and a promise of the ultimate sacrifice. We can live with ever-present confidence that our Good Shepherd loves us so much that he will die to protect us. In both word pictures, Jesus as a shepherd and Jesus as a sheep, the end is the same: because he gave his life, we are alive. All praise to Jesus for his indescribable grace!

The Gate. Let's take another step into the world of shepherds and sheep. In Jesus' day, protecting sheep from being eaten, stolen, or lost was a full-time job. Lots of people were in the sheep-care business. All of them knew that one of the best ways to keep sheep from wandering or getting eaten or being stolen was to corral them and lock the gate. A secure gate was a deterrent to predators and thieves and robbers.

Once again, Jesus reaches into his culture and common understanding and makes a comparison. "I am the gate for the sheep" (John 10:7–10). He says, "Whoever enters through me will be saved." Wrap your mind around this powerful picture. He is the protecting gate that opens and invites people (sheep) into his place of protection and life.

The Resurrection and the Life. If you do a reflective reading through the four gospels, you will find many more names for Jesus. Many of them relate to his saving power and love. For our study here, we will look at just one more descriptive title for Jesus. He called himself "the resurrection and the life" (John 11:25). He made this declaration right before he called Lazarus out of the grave after Lazarus had been buried for four days (John 11:38–44). We who walk with Jesus know the one who rose from the grave and who promises to raise us up with him. We also know that our Savior has the power to raise up all who place their faith in him.

What's in a name? Do these titles really matter to our lives? In the ancient world, names and titles mattered, and they still do today. As you think about sharing the message and good news of Jesus, remember that he is the Messiah, the Bread of Heaven, the Living Water, the Light of the World, the Lamb of God, the Good Shepherd, the Gate, and the Resurrection and the Life. We who know his lifesaving names should share them with others.

Why Did Jesus Come?

Just as the *who* matters, so does the *why*. We have taken time to clarify who Jesus is. Now we turn our attention to the question, why did he come? The why actually connects to a who. All through the Gospels, Jesus and others reveal the reason he came. Although there were many reasons for the incarnation, the bullseye is all about a who. And that who is you!

Of course, it is not just about you. Jesus came for all who would believe and receive his grace. But the Lord of Glory, who emptied himself to come as one of us, did it for people. For his beloved. For you.

Jesus came to reveal the love and grace of God. As trinitarian Christians, we understand that the Father, the Son, and the Spirit are united in being. This means that the love we see in Jesus is a perfect reflection of our heavenly Father. In possibly the most familiar passage in the Bible, John 3:16, we are reminded that the initiator of the plan of salvation is God the Father. "For God so loved the world that he gave his one and only Son, that whoever believes in him shall not perish but have eternal life." Why did Jesus come? Because God loves us!

Jesus came to preach and bring the good news of the kingdom. Jesus was a king, and wherever he went, his kingdom was there. When he came to our world, his kingdom, in some form, came with him. Jesus preached about his kingdom over and over (Matt. 4:17; 6:33; 19:14; Mark 1:15; Luke 12:32; John 3:3). Many of his parables focused on his kingdom. Much of his preaching centered on the good news of the kingdom he was bringing.

Right after Jesus was tempted by the devil in the wilderness, he went to the city of Nazareth, where he had grown up. On the Sabbath, Jesus went to the synagogue. When he stood up to read the Scriptures, they handed him the scroll of Isaiah. Jesus let his eyes scan down the text until he found the place where these words were written:

> "The Spirit of the Lord is on me,
>   because he has anointed me
>   to proclaim good news to the poor.

He has sent me to proclaim freedom for the prisoners
    and recovery of sight for the blind,
to set the oppressed free,
    to proclaim the year of the Lord's favor."

—Luke 4:18–19

Good news for the poor, freedom for prisoners, sight for the blind, freedom for the oppressed, and the favor of God. This gives a taste of the kind of kingdom Jesus came to bring.

Jesus came to call people to repentance. Our Lord delights in pouring out blessings beyond our comprehension. Yet he will never look the other way and ignore our sin. Jesus does not sweep our rebellion under some heavenly carpet and act like we have not fallen. Like a loving parent, he confronts our wrongs and calls us to turn from them. He offers a new path of life, health, and joy. We get to decide whether we will accept his invitation and walk in his ways. At the end of Jesus' first sermon after his wilderness temptation, we read that he began to preach, "Repent, for the kingdom of heaven has come near" (Matt. 4:17). When a loving parent sees their child running toward a busy street, they scream, "Stop!" When a loving God sees his beloved children destroying their lives and eternity in the cesspool of sin, he calls out, "Repent! Turn around! Follow my ways!"

Jesus came to save sinners. Jesus did not come for the pure, pristine, and perfect people of this world. (By the way, there are no such people!) Our Lord came for broken, sinful, rebellious, trapped, hopeless, bitter everyday people like you and me. The apostle Paul stated emphatically that "all have sinned and fall short of the glory of God" (Rom. 3:23). And as has been said by many people before us, "All means all, or it means nothing at all!" Every human being to walk this planet, except Jesus, has been infected by the sin virus.

A casual review of the people Jesus reached out to, loved, and forgave makes it clear that he came for everyone who will receive him. Tax collectors and sinners, you are welcome (Matt. 9:9–13)! Broken and disheartened, stand, walk, and be forgiven (Luke 5:17–26)! Sinful woman pushed out of pleasant society, come near and be cleansed of your sordid past (Luke 7:36–50)! Woman with five failed marriages and living with another man, come and worship me, right here and right now (John 4:1–26)! Look in the mirror: Jesus loves that sinner. Think about friends and family members who are hardhearted and far from the Savior. Jesus came for them too!

Jesus came to suffer and die. The prophets revealed the truth long before the Son of God took on flesh. He would be broken, pierced, and crushed, and our iniquities would be heaped on him (Isa. 53:4–6). Our gentle Savior and the one who loves us most came to offer himself as a once-for-all sacrifice for our sins. Every time we partake of communion, we remember this spiritual reality. The cup is poured out as a sign of his blood shed. From the site of his scourging, through the streets of Jerusalem, up the hill called Calvary, and on the cross, Jesus poured out his life for us. The payment was enough for all of our wrongs. The bread of communion reminds us of his body beaten, punctured, and disfigured so that he might put the fragmented pieces of our lives back together. His life for ours. An infinite sacrifice, offered by an infinite Savior, to cover our offenses against an infinite God.

Jesus came to conquer sin, death, hell, and the enemy. The resurrection is the divine exclamation point after the crucifixion. All that Jesus promised was authenticated when he stood up and walked out of the grave. "Where, O death, is your victory? Where, O death, is your sting?" (1 Cor. 15:55). In Jesus Christ, and through his resurrection, death is dead! The enemy is defeated. The sting of sin is gone. We cry out with the apostle, "But thanks be to God! He gives us the victory through our Lord Jesus Christ" (1 Cor. 15:57). The resurrection of Jesus changes everything.

Jesus came to call disciples. In Christ, salvation is ours, the power of sin is broken, and heaven is our home. All praise to God!

But the story does not stop there. Jesus came to build his church, form a family, and bring his light to the world. This happens when we hear the call of Jesus: "Whoever wants to be my disciple must deny themselves and take up their cross and follow me. For whoever wants to save their life will lose it, but whoever loses their life for me will find it" (Matt. 16:24–25). Salvation comes when we accept the gift of grace offered by Jesus through his sacrifice on the cross. Sanctification is a lifelong journey with Jesus, surrendering to his will each moment of the day.

If we are going to join Jesus on his mission of seeking and saving the lost in this world, we must first confess our sins and receive his grace. Jesus becomes our Savior! Then we take his hand, follow his ways, obey his Word, and grow to be more like him. He becomes our Lord.

CHAPTER 23

Sweaty Palms and a Dry Mouth: Facing Fear

Dan and Sheila both love Jesus. They believe the Bible and pray regularly for friends and neighbors who are not yet saved by God's grace. One of their greatest desires is for people to come to faith in Jesus. One of their deepest joys is when family members and friends finally receive the grace of God and come home through faith in the Savior.

Sheila is bold, verbal, and has spiritual conversations with nonbelievers frequently and naturally. Dan is serious about his faith and lives it out. At the same time, talking about what he believes and entering conversations about Jesus makes him nervous.

After a church service where the theme was all about sharing faith with others, Dan and Sheila sat down to have lunch and talk about the sermon. Sheila said, "Dan, I know how deep your faith is. I know you believe the gospel. I can see how you love people and want them to meet Jesus. After today's sermon, do you feel ready to talk more about your faith?"

Dan thought for a moment and replied, "I am ready. I feel

equipped, prepared, and committed to engage in thoughtful conversations about Jesus." He went on, "But every time I am about to tell my story of coming to Jesus or to ask someone about their faith journey, something happens. Each time I sense the Holy Spirit prompting me to talk about Jesus or share the gospel, my mouth gets as dry as cotton and my palms get sweaty."

Sheila considered Dan's dilemma, and then a big smile lit up her face. "I have a solution! When your mouth starts to get dry and your palms get sweaty, just lick your hands and start talking about Jesus."[32]

The truth is, almost everyone gets nervous when it comes time to open their mouths and talk about faith. Various surveys and studies reveal that between one and three percent of Christians are gifted in evangelism. If you do the math, 97 to 99 percent of Christians feel some kind of fear, nervousness, or caution having spiritual conversations or sharing the message of Jesus.

Jesus Called His Followers to Share His Good News

God made us and knows us better than we know ourselves. We can trust him. Christians are called to be like our Savior—we bear his name. We are to follow his example and respond to his call on our lives. Jesus sent his disciples out to share the message of his grace and model the power and presence of God in this world. The twelve apostles were sent to proclaim the kingdom of God and share the good news (Luke 9:1–9). When our Savior sent out seventy-two of his followers, he said that "the harvest is plentiful, but the workers are few" (Luke 10:2). Before Jesus sent them off, he "comforted" them with these words: "I am sending you out like lambs among wolves" (Luke 10:3) Talk about the potential for dry mouths and sweaty palms! Jesus knows the mission is dangerous, costly, and fear inducing, but he still sends us.

Jesus Painted Powerful Pictures of Who We Are

The world tries to define who we are, and the enemy of our souls wants to sow lies and deception. Jesus countered this by painting pictures that will lock into our minds and calm our souls. As you grow in your commitment to follow Jesus on his grand mission, remember who you are.

You are a fisher of people. The early disciples heard the call, and so should we. Followers of Jesus are out on the waters of this world with the goal of seeing people caught up in the love, grace, and glory of God (Matt. 4:18–22; Mark 1:16–20). We can spend our days doing all we can to discover how people will respond to the invitation Jesus extends to all lost people. If they reject what is offered, we don't quit. We ask new questions, share fresh stories of God's grace, and pray for new opportunities to have spiritual conversations.[33]

You offer living water. We live in a world filled with people who are dying of thirst. When someone becomes so parched that they can't take it anymore, they will drink almost anything. People gulp down the filthy "refreshments" the world offers and don't even notice it is killing them. Jesus offers living water, pure and clean. Here is the staggering truth: Jesus' water flows through you (John 4:13–14). When he became your Savior and leader, your spiritual thirst was quenched. On top of that, you became a conduit of his living water. Delight that you are a fountain overflowing with the refreshment only Jesus can provide.

You are light in this world. The moon reflects the light of the sun. On a dark night, there are times it is so bright, we can walk safely with no flashlight. Jesus is the Light of the World. He so fills us and reflects off us that his light can be seen in our dark world. Jesus said that his light can shine so brightly through us that the world will see and give glory to God in heaven (Matt. 5:14–16).

When you think of yourself, don't believe the lies of the enemy. Remember that Jesus said, "You are the light of the world."

You are the salt of the earth. Salt creates thirst! This is why restaurants are willing to give out "free" popcorn, nuts, and chips. These snacks are a stealthy way of getting salt into your mouth. The goal is to create thirst so you will buy drinks. Jesus is the Living Water, and when his disciples are in the world, they create thirst for Jesus. Our Lord said, "You are the salt of the earth" (Matt. 5:13). As you live out your faith with transparency and joy, others will watch and thirst for the refreshment that can be found in Jesus alone.

Who am I? Ask that question boldly. Then let Jesus answer it. You are a fisher of people, a conduit of living water, the light of the world, and the salt of the earth. Never forget it!

I Can Do This!

Jesus not only affirmed who we are as his disciples, but he gave compelling direction for what we are called to do. When it comes to the gospel and reaching out to lost people in natural ways, Jesus made it clear. There are some things we all can do.

We are to scatter the seed of the gospel. Jesus shared a parable to help us understand our role as seed sowers (Matt. 13:1–23). What is fascinating is that the sower in this story was not like any farmer in Jesus' day. Seed was expensive and precious. It was planted strategically and carefully. Yet this farmer scattered seed everywhere! Weedy ground—scatter some seed. Hard-packed paths—scatter. Rocky places—cast some seed. Good soil—throw seed.

Why would Jesus give this strange story as an example of sharing the good news of the kingdom? Because we are not smart enough to determine the right soil or the perfect timing. So Jesus removes those obstacles. He calls us to scatter the seed of the gospel everywhere we go, all the time, no matter what the soil conditions seem to be. This removes the mystery of our needing to figure out when we should scatter seed. It is always the right time!

We are to join Jesus in finding lost sheep. Jesus told another parable that helps us see how a disciple follows him into the practice of organic outreach (evangelism). God desires that no person should perish. We are called to identify wandering sheep. This is any person who has not yet embraced Jesus as their Savior and leader. We are to see these people as wandering and join Jesus on his mission of finding them with his love (Matt. 18:10–14). Make a list of lost sheep you know, and pray for courage to partner with the Good Shepherd as he searches for them.

We are to love our neighbors. Our first calling is to love God with all we have and are. Next, Jesus made it clear that loving people as we want to be loved should be of paramount importance to a disciple (Matt. 22:39). Organic outreach is founded on the assurance that God loves every lost sheep. Once we are found by our Shepherd, we learn to love people as he does. Pause to invite the Holy Spirit to grow your love for people in your life who are far from Jesus. Even the difficult, resistant, and hostile folks.

Ask yourself, "Can I learn to scatter the seed of the gospel as a lifestyle? Am I willing to see people as lost, lonely, and loved sheep, just the way Jesus does? Will I have the courage to love my neighbors, even when they are acting in unlovely ways?" These are things every Christian can do as we walk in the power and leading of the Spirit.

Practical Ways to Lick Your Palms (without Actually Licking Them)

We can know who we are in Christ and identify what he wants us to do, and still fail to act on Jesus' invitation to make disciples of all people. What we need are some simple steps to move us forward on the joyous journey of sharing faith.

Name and face your fears. "I don't want to look bad." "I worry I will mess up and say something wrong." "This could cost me a friendship." "I could be rejected by others if I am too vocal about my love for Jesus." The list goes on. One way to move forward in sharing our faith is to acknowledge our fears. If we don't, the devil will lie, blow up our fears, and paralyze us. When we admit our fears to God, he can speak truth, set us free from lies, and give us boldness. When we admit our fears to other Christians, they can give us perspective, share wisdom, and offer accountability to help us live with evangelistic boldness.

Embrace your fears. For most of history, people have known that running from fears is not a wise course of action. Ignoring or avoiding fear does not make us more mature. It does not move the work of Jesus forward. Wise people take the hand of God and step into his will, even when it scares them.

Picture the people of Israel as they stood on the bank of the Jordan River while it was at flood stage (Joshua 3). God gave them explicit instructions. The leaders were to step into the swollen river while carrying the massive and heavy ark of the covenant. This could have seemed like a death sentence. God promised to stop the rushing waters after they stepped in, not before. If you don't know how the story ended, read it today. You will be inspired.

Check your theology. Some have adopted errant theology that peddles a soft universalism. They comfort themselves with a false belief that all people will go to heaven. They ignore passages that clearly affirm Jesus as the only way to salvation (John 14:6). They avoid biblical teaching on hell and judgment. If you have fallen into compromised theology that gives the impression that God will sweep every single person into heaven, take time to read some biblical teaching that will move you outward with the message of Jesus' love, truth, and grace.

Stop passing the buck. "I'm not an evangelist." "I serve Jesus and his church in other ways. I will leave outreach to the more gifted."

"I'm just too shy and quiet." It is easy to expect God to use someone else to share the good news of Jesus. The problem is, God has placed each of us right where we are. You have a unique personal journey to and with Jesus. You have a temperament that is perfect to reach certain people. You have a calling to be salt and light. Decide today. No more passing the buck. Commit to engage in God's epic mission of reaching lost sheep.

Check your schedule. Look at the next week and month of your life. If you have significant time to be with friends and family members who are not Christians, great! If you are jammed up with church responsibilities and all your time is devoted to other Jesus followers, cancel some stuff. Make sure you have time, every week, to be with people God wants to reach with his grace. Then pray that your time with each person makes space for God to show up and shine his light through you.

Find an organic-outreach mentor. Take time this week to identify someone you know who is farther down the road in living the growth marker of organic outreach. Ask if they will take your hand, in a formal or casual way, and teach you what they know about sharing God's love and the message of Jesus. Watch them, learn from them, and follow their example. If you dare, invite them to pray with you for opportunities to connect more closely with nonbelievers. Have them keep you accountable to follow through as you walk with Jesus on his mission to seek and save the lost.

Count the cost. Ask God to help you see that whatever the cost you might pay to share the truth and grace of Jesus, it is worth it! Jesus told his followers that no one who left loved ones and the security of their occupation for the sake of the gospel would fail to receive a hundred times back in this life and eternity (Mark 10:29–31). It is hard to know exactly what this means, but it is clear that Jesus wanted his followers to know that it will all be worth it.

As Jesus was drawing near the end of his ministry on this earth, he told his followers that the road would be hard. He spoke of persecution, prison, political confrontation, betrayal by family and friends, and even martyrdom (Luke 21:5–28). He also promised to be with them and said, "Stand firm, and you will win life" (Luke 21:19).

We all will have moments when our mouths get dry and our hands get sweaty. The call to share the good news of Jesus always comes with a cost. This should not surprise us—it cost our Lord his life. But there is no better adventure, no higher calling, and no greater joy than seeing a lost sheep come home to the Good Shepherd.

4 Generation Challenge (2-2-2)

In my family, I (Kevin) have watched the beauty of organic outreach cross four generations of people. Three of those generations were siblings. For one final time, watch the power of Christians clasping hands and taking seriously the call to discipleship.

When my sister Gretchen became a follower of Jesus, she was changed. Of course, she was still shy by temperament, but she had a new boldness. She prayed for her parents and siblings. She tried to be a witness to her faith and became a fisher of people, light, salt, and a pipeline of Jesus' living water. She really did! She invited me to her youth group again and again, even when I gave harsh and mean-spirited negative responses. Gretchen kept showing me the love of Jesus. She took my hand even when I refused it and did not recognize what was going on. With time, her influence, along with some godly young men she introduced me to, brought fruit. The seeds Gretchen and her friends scattered took root. I became a Christian.

Immediately, I joined Gretchen in seeking to take the hands of our other siblings and help them toward Jesus. Our younger brother, Jason, was highly resistant. Over the coming years, he pushed back against our efforts with increasing intellectual argument and occasional hostility. But Gretchen and I, along with many others, kept praying for Jason. We shared our faith with him as often as we could. We gave him books on apologetics, shared music with a Christian message, and extended many invitations to places he could hear the gospel and meet some pretty cool Jesus followers. He eventually began dating a young Christian woman named Mindy, and she joined us on the journey of helping Jason learn about Jesus and open his heart to the Savior. With time, by the grace of Jesus and the power of the Holy Spirit, Jason became a Christian.

Of course, the story does not end there. Jason and Mindy have six beautiful children. They are taking the hands of each of them and sharing the love and good news of Jesus. It has been a delight to watch Jason and Mindy build a Jesus-centered life and home. They do not (and could not) force faith on any of their kids. But they model it, teach it, and pray faithfully that each of their children will grow to love and follow Jesus.

Can you see how hands locked together in discipleship can change the world? Gretchen reached out to me (sibling to sibling), I partnered with many others in reaching out to Jason (sibling to sibling), Jason and Mindy are faithfully locking hands with each of their children and discipling them (parents to children). That is four generations of hands locked in organic discipleship.

CHAPTER 24

The Thing We Say We Value Most, We Do the Least

Over the past three decades, we have had the honor of training church leaders in organic outreach. All around the United States and the world, people tell us the same thing. In our travels, teaching, and partnership with global church leaders, two themes come up over and over again.

1. "We believe the gospel and want to reach out and see people come to faith in Jesus." This is almost universal. From denominational leaders in the US, to movement leaders in New Zealand, to pastors in El Salvador, to passionate Christians all over the globe, the message is the same. We believe in evangelism. We are committed to it. We long to see the good news of Jesus transform lives now and for eternity.

2. "We just don't do outreach very well!" In some cases, the message is, "We don't do evangelism at all." From individual church members to pastors, to denominational and global leaders, we have lost count of the number of heartrending

conversations we've had and confessions we've heard. Leaders pull us aside and admit that the thing they believe in the most is also what they do the least. This usually applies to their personal lives as well as the ministries they lead or serve.

How can it be that so many faithful followers of Jesus don't engage in sharing the good news that saved them and changed their lives? Why do so many churches have a mission statement that declares their commitment to evangelism, but they don't practice it? How can we take steps to align our actions with our stated beliefs about evangelism?

This is the central purpose of this book! Good discipleship leads to a lifestyle of evangelistic outreach. When we look at Jesus and see how he loved the Scriptures, prayed with passion, encouraged worship, served with humility, gave with generosity, nurtured community, and called people to faith, we have a model of the Christian life. Then when we engage in each of these aspects of spiritual growth, we mature and become more like our Savior. As this happens, we reach out more, we share our faith with greater courage, and we make space in our day for relationships with those who need to know the amazing grace of Jesus.

When Walt Bennett left the business world to become the CEO of Organic Outreach International, he and his wife, Liz, realized that they needed to engage in more personal outreach. They were faithful and committed followers of Jesus, but their growing discipleship was not leading them to a lifestyle of outreach. Walt wanted to live what he was going to lead, and Liz was excited to partner with her husband in exploring new ways to reach out right where they lived. They had been living in their neighborhood for almost six years and knew exactly three families out of the twenty-two in their vicinity. The truth was, they did not know their neighbors and were not having a spiritual impact in their neighborhood.

Walt and Liz came to understand that their call as Christians was more than just going to church, reading their Bibles, and praying. They were called to reach the lost right where God placed them. They knew something had to change. With this in mind, and after prayer and conversation, Walt and Liz knocked on the doors of eighteen of the twenty-two homes around them. (The other four homes were not occupied because the people came only seasonally.) They invited each neighbor to a BBQ at their house, explaining that they had lived in the neighborhood for six years, knew almost no one, and suspected most others were in the same boat. At least one person from the eighteen homes showed up on the day of the event. Some of their neighbors were meeting each other for the first time after having lived in the neighborhood for many years, and in one case, for more than twenty-four years!

This was only the first step. They followed up by establishing Firepit Friday. One or two times each month, they invited everyone to stop by their home, where they would have a portable firepit at the end of their driveway with all the fixin's for roasted hot dogs. Everyone was welcome to come by anytime between 5:30 and 9:00 p.m. Over the coming years, these gatherings were a focal point of the neighborhood, and Walt and Liz forged deep and lasting relationships with everyone who came.

Each of these relationships developed differently, but in every one, Walt and Liz naturally shared the love of Christ with their neighbors through stories, encouragement, and actions. Walt was able to encourage one husband in how to share Jesus one final time with his wife, who was dying of cancer. This neighbor came to Walt two weeks later to let him know his wife had just passed away, but he knew he would be seeing her in heaven. Walt was privileged to preside at her memorial service and, at her request, to share the gospel with all those who attended. It is amazing what God can do when we seek authentic relationships and shine the light of Jesus in organic ways.

Take the Call Personally!

Every Christian, church leader, and denominational executive needs to hear the mission of Jesus as a call to them personally. Too often we affirm the gospel of Jesus in a vague and general sense and feel convicted that Christians should engage in evangelism. What we fail to do is recognize that Jesus calls every one of us to shine his light, scatter his seed, be the salt of the earth, and put our faith into words that affirm our actions. Notice what the risen Jesus said to his followers right before he ascended to heaven: "Then Jesus came to them and said, 'All authority in heaven and on earth has been given to me. Therefore go and make disciples of all nations, baptizing them in the name of the Father and of the Son and of the Holy Spirit, and teaching them to obey everything I have commanded you. And surely I am with you always, to the very end of the age'" (Matt. 28:18–20).

Note how Jesus begins and ends this Great Commission. He starts where we should: focusing on his glory and authority. Jesus has all power and authority on earth and in heaven. He ends by assuring us of his presence with us now and for eternity. We must recognize what comes in the middle of this commission. Us. Disciples of Jesus.

Yes, Jesus has all authority. Absolutely, he is with us always. Certain of these two things, *we* are to go and make disciples of all nations. We are to baptize new believers. We are to teach all that Jesus commanded. We are to go on mission with Jesus and partner in evangelism and discipleship.

One Way to Heaven, but Many Ways to Share the Gospel

One of the greatest deterrents to Christians engaging in organic outreach is the errant belief that there is just one way to do evangelism.

Most Christians who think this way do not see themselves as fitting that narrow mold. Nothing could be farther from the truth! There is only one gospel, one Savior, and one way to heaven. But there are countless ways to walk with a person toward the Savior. Jesus himself was a powerful model of this reality.

In the Gospel of John, Jesus encountered two dramatically different people in back-to-back chapters. In John chapter 3, the Lord spends time with a man named Nicodemus. In the next chapter, Jesus has an extensive theological conversation with a woman at a well. These two people lived in vastly different worlds. Yet both of them placed their faith in Jesus and accepted him as their Messiah.

Nicodemus was a powerful man. He was Jewish. He served on the high court of Israel, and was wealthy and influential. He was seen as righteous and as an example of religious purity. He met Jesus at night. The woman in chapter 4 of John's Gospel was a Samaritan, powerless, poor, outcast, and known for her sinful lifestyle. She met Jesus in the heat of the day. These two people could not have been more different.

As you read about Jesus' interactions with both of these spiritually hungry people, it becomes clear that the Savior was not using some memorized religious script. He clearly had not taken a class on six steps to easy conversion. Each conversation was as unique as the person Jesus met. Our Lord did not launch into a speech but engaged in thoughtful conversation. The interests and longings of Nicodemus and the woman were different, so the conversations were not the same.

What is important for us to recognize is that Jesus talked about faith with both. Each conversation ended up revealing who Jesus was and the need for salvation. Both Nicodemus and the woman found someone who would listen to them. Jesus let them ask their questions, share their needs, and articulate their longings. We should learn to do the same.

Organic outreach is all about sharing faith in a way that is natural for us. It should also feel comfortable for the people to whom we are speaking. Sharing the message of Jesus should not freak us out or drive spiritual seekers away. Every encounter is unique, and we can love, listen, pray, and share in a way that fits the person and the situation.

We have written and created a number of resources to help Christians do exactly that.[34]

The Power of Your Story

One of the most organic ways to share our faith is telling our stories. Every one of us has a story of our conversion. This is telling another person about how we came to faith in Jesus and the difference he has made in our lives. When we do this, we talk about who Jesus is, what he did for us on the cross, how he rose from the dead, and why we received his grace and forgiveness for our sins. We also communicate how our relationship with Jesus has transformed our lives for the better. As people listen to our stories, they hear the gospel.

In addition to our conversion stories, we have stories of God's presence and power in our lives. These stories are fresh and new all the time. Since God is real, alive, and present, we all have fresh stories about how he is moving right now.

As we read the four gospels, we learn about people who came to faith in Jesus, were transformed, and then told their stories right away. The woman who met Jesus at the well embraced him as the Messiah and Savior. She then hurried back to her town to tell everyone to come and meet the one who "told me everything I ever did" (John 4:39). Her story of encountering Jesus' grace and acceptance had an impact on others, who also placed their faith in him. A man Jesus freed from demonic possession (Mark 5:1–20) went and told people in his city what Jesus had done for him. A blind man who had been touched by Jesus' healing power was confronted by the religious leaders. They had a warped perspective on Jesus and called him a sinner because he healed on the wrong day of the week. The healed man said, "Whether he is a sinner or not, I don't know. One thing I do know. I was blind but now I see" (John 9:25).

What is interesting about all of these people sharing their testimony is that they did it in a matter of hours or days after becoming followers of Jesus. So often we believe it is necessary to take classes and be trained to share our faith. While we are huge fans of training for evangelism, any follower of Jesus can tell their story of faith right away.

What is so powerful about a Christian sharing their testimony is that it is their experience with Jesus. In our world today, people often shy away from absolute and objective truth. Although Christians believe in absolutes and have lots of truth to share, our stories are accounts of what happened to us. This resonates with many people today. As we boldly tell our stories, most people will be fascinated and curious.

When a Christian shares, "I was lonely and did not feel loved, but when I received Jesus as my Savior, everything changed. I now know I belong to him, am loved, and have a family!" Who can argue with that? When a Jesus follower says, "I had no real purpose in my life or driving passion to get me out of the bed each morning. But now I have meaning and direction, and I wake up with excitement and joy," who can question that? When a longtime believer explains, "In my time of need and uncertainty, God showed up and provided in amazing and miraculous ways," people become curious and wonder whether God might be real.

If you have placed your faith in Jesus, you have a story to tell about his saving power, love, and presence with you. Tell that story and share how receiving Jesus as the one who forgives your sins and leads your life has made all the difference in the world. Tell many stories about answered prayers, surprising heavenly provision, comfort in hard times, and direction in the darkness. Each one of these helps people see that God is moving and present in this world and in your life.

The Power of His Story

People love stories. As a follower of Jesus, you have a story to tell that everyone needs to hear. It is the best news in the history of the world. It is true. This story can transform lives, heal hearts, wash away sin, infuse hope, and change the world. It is the story of Jesus.

Every disciple should be ready and able to articulate the simple message of Jesus in a way that is memorable and makes sense to any child, teen, or adult who is willing to listen. We have distilled the story of Jesus down to eight words. If you can remember these four pairs of words, you can tell the most compelling story in human history. Here are the words, with brief explanations:

- *God's love:* There is a loving God who longs to bring his wandering children home.
- *Our problem:* We have all sinned and are under judgment that separates us from God.
- *God's solution:* Jesus' sacrificial death can remove our sin and restore us to God.
- *Our response:* We are invited to accept Jesus' gift of grace and be saved.

To make it even easier to remember these eight words, the first letters of each pair spell GOGO. The risen Lord Jesus calls his followers to GO and make disciples of all people.

Of course, these eight words are not the whole story. They simply help us organize our thoughts as we tell others the good news of Jesus. We could write many chapters to expand these ideas and help you learn to tell the story of Jesus with clarity, passion, and conviction. We have provided sources for the best places to go deeper into this topic.[35] For now, we encourage you to commit these eight words to memory (it should not take more than a few minutes), and then practice articulating the story of Jesus using these four simple ideas as your pathway through it.

Take training seriously. If your church offers a learning experience about understanding the gospel and sharing your faith, jump into it! Don't hesitate. The apostle Peter exhorts disciples of Jesus to "always be prepared to give an answer to everyone who asks you to give the reason for the hope that you have" (1 Peter 3:15). If you want to be equipped to winsomely share your faith with people you love, we provide free videos and resources on the Organic Outreach International website.[36] There is nothing more important than knowing the story of Jesus and being ready to share it with clarity, conviction, and grace.

Keep evangelism and discipleship connected. As you pray for opportunities to share your stories and the good news of Jesus, be ready to walk with people to the cross and then beyond. Evangelism and discipleship are married in the heart of God. Take the hand of someone far from Jesus and begin helping them walk toward the Savior. When, by the power of God's Spirit, they come to faith, that is not the end of the journey. It is the start of a new chapter.

Be ready to continue holding their hand and help them take steps forward in all seven of the spiritual growth markers. As you see this new believer growing in faith, challenge them to take the hand of someone else so they can experience the joy of helping another person walk toward Jesus. There is no better way to live. This is the journey of a disciple.

No credit and no blame. As we follow Jesus and seek to reach out to people who are far from the Savior, we have to remember that we do not have the power to save anyone. Jesus came from heaven, gave his life on the cross, died in our places, and rose from the grave. Only he can save. We have the honor and privilege of scattering the seed of the gospel, telling his story, praying with passion, and inviting people to know Jesus.[37]

When someone comes to faith, we don't get the credit. That belongs to Jesus. We also do not live with the weight of blame if a person remains hardhearted and refuses God's grace. We are partners with Jesus in his Great Commission, but he is always the senior partner!

Remember, it is never too late. Don't give up! If you have been praying for someone to open their heart to Jesus for a month, a year, a decade, or forty-four years, don't stop. God is at work, and he desires their salvation more than you do. Keep loving. Never stop serving in the name of Jesus. Lift up passionate prayers. Speak words of blessing. Tell the story of Jesus. Pray some more. Open your heart, arms, schedule, home, and church to people far from God. If you ever feel you are growing weary, read these words from Scripture and press on, for the glory of God and for the sake of the world: "But do not forget this one thing, dear friends: With the Lord a day is like a thousand years, and a thousand years are like a day. The Lord is not slow in keeping his promise, as some understand slowness. Instead he is patient with you, not wanting anyone to perish, but everyone to come to repentance" (2 Peter 3:8–9).

Closing Thoughts

The Joyful Journey of a Disciple:
Upward, Inward, Outward

Nothing is more meaningful and joy filled than drawing close to the God who made us and loves us. When the fruit of the Spirit is growing in us and forming our character, we become more like Jesus. As we join in the great procession of Christians through history and lock hands with people in front of us and behind us, we become true disciples. We learn from those who are more mature. We take consistent steps of growth. We help others go deeper in faith. And we teach them to take the hand of the next generation and do the same. This is the pathway of organic disciples.

Each day, our journey is upward to God as worshipers, inward toward his family in community, and outward to the world with the gospel. Every one of the markers of spiritual maturity connects us to God, makes us more like Jesus, and propels us out to love the lost sheep that Jesus came to save.

Follow Jesus. Enjoy the climb. Never travel alone. Lock hands and press on for the glory of God!

Notes

1. For more information on this topic, see the book *Organic Outreach for Ordinary People: Sharing Good News Naturally.*
2. To learn more about sharing faith with your family, read *Organic Outreach for Families: Turning Your Home into a Lighthouse.*
3. *Organic Outreach for Churches*, chap. 1, "Loving God: Without This, Nothing Else Matters."
4. You can search the Bible section at Zondervan.com for one-year Bibles, chronological Bibles, and other resources.
5. You can find resources for The Big Picture of the Bible on the *Organic Disciples* section of the Organic Outreach website: organicoutreach.org.
6. You can find resources for *The Story* at Zondervan.com and at Shoreline.church. (See sermon resources for *The Story*.)
7. You can find a list of questions on the *Organic Disciples* section of the Organic Outreach website: organicoutreach.org.
8. For more information on the Voice of the Martyrs and the story of Richard Wurmbrand, go to https://www.persecution.com/.
9. Read *Organic Outreach for Churches*, chap. 2, "Loving the World: What Are You Willing to Sacrifice?"
10. For more information on Dr. Charles Van Engen, search the websites for Latin American Ministries and Fuller Theological Seminary.
11. A great resource for deeper study is Norman L. Geisler and Frank

Turek, *I Don't Have Enough Faith to be an Atheist* (Wheaton, IL: Crossway, 2004), www.backtothebible.org.

12. Not only is *Praying with Eyes Wide Open* a book (Grand Rapids, Baker: 2017), but free ministry resources are available at https://sherryharney.com/.

13. Learn more about this by reading Sherry Harney with Kevin Harney, *Praying with Eyes Wide Open: A Life-Changing Way to Talk with God* (Grand Rapids: Baker, 2017), chap. 10, "Honest to God."

14. See https://BlessEveryHome.com.

15. Learn more about Organic Outreach International training online and in person at organicoutreach.org.

16. You can find resources for a Salvation Prayer on the *Organic Disciples* section of the Organic Outreach website: organicoutreach.org.

17. Learn more about the Organic Outreach trilogy of books at zondervan.com or organicoutreach.org.

18. *Organic Outreach for Ordinary People*, chap. 6, "The Unseen Work: Praying for People," and chap. 7, "The Wonder of Encounter: Praying with People."

19. The Athanasian Creed focuses on the two natures of Christ (fully divine and fully man) and on the Trinity. It is not used as often in worship services because of its highly theological framework, but it is rich and worth reading if you are not familiar with it.

20. *Organic Outreach for Ordinary People*, chap. 8, "Incarnational Living."

21. You can find resources for leading a Level 4 Gospel Sunday at your church on the *Organic Disciples* section of the Organic Outreach website: organicoutreach.org.

22. *Finding a Church You Can Love and Loving the Church You've Found* by Kevin Harney and Sherry Harney. This is a helpful resource for finding the right church and then learning to be part of the body of Christ.

23. *Organic Outreach for Ordinary People*, chap. 10, "The Work of the Holy Spirit."

24. Find ideas for sharing the gospel in clear and practical ways in Kevin G. Harney, *Organic Outreach for Ordinary People: Sharing Good News Naturally* (Grand Rapids: Zondervan, 2009), chap. 13.

25. Find Good Neighbor ministry ideas at https://shoreline.church
/the-good-neighbor/.
26. *Reckless Faith*, chap. 4, "Reckless Generosity."
27. For some of our best ideas on growing in generosity, see Kevin G.
Harney, *Seismic Shifts: The Little Changes That Make a Big
Difference in Your Life* (Grand Rapids: Zondervan, 2008), chaps.
13–15.
28. Books about contentment and finances: Jeff Manion, *Satisfied:
Discovering Contentment in a World of Consumption* (Grand Rapids:
Zondervan, 2014), and Dave Ramsey, *Financial Peace: Restoring
Financial Hope to You and Your Family* (New York: Viking, 1997).
29. Randy Frazee, in his book *Making Room for Life: Trading Chaotic
Lifestyles for Connected Relationships* (Grand Rapids: Zondervan,
2003), gives some great ideas for developing community and
conversation around a table.
30. Find ideas for making your church a place that is welcoming to
spiritually curious people in Kevin G. Harney, *Organic Outreach for
Churches: Infusing Evangelistic Passion in Your Local Congregation*
(Grand Rapids: Zondervan, 2018).
31. *Organic Outreach for Churches*, chap. 12, "Telling Your Story."
32. We have no idea whether this story is true. We have heard it used
in a variety of outreach contexts and don't know the source. But it is
funny and makes a point!
33. Gregory Koukl, *Tactics: A Game Plan for Discussing Your Christian
Faith*.
34. You can find resources on the *Organic Disciples* section of the
Organic Outreach website: organicoutreach.org.
35. You can find more resources for the gospel GOGO in Kevin G. Harney,
Organic Outreach for Ordinary People: Sharing Good News Naturally
(Grand Rapids: Zondervan, 2009), and on the *Organic Disciples* section
of the Organic Outreach website: organicoutreach.org.
36. Organicoutreach.org.
37. *Organic Outreach for Ordinary People*, chap. 10, "The Work of the
Holy Spirit."

OrganicOutreach

INTERNATIONAL

Through training, coaching, and provision of resources, Organic Outreach International is committed to helping denominations, national groups, regional movements, parachurch organizations and churches around the world infuse the DNA of their ministries and congregations with a passion for natural evangelism. We offer online and onsite training sessions ranging from half-day introductory seminars to two-day intensive trainings. For churches and movements that are directly engaging in organic outreach, we provide a collaborative coaching experience for small groups (cohorts) of pastors and outreach influence team leaders through a combination of online work and monthly video conferencing.

For churches and organizations engaging in organic outreach, we provide free resources on our website. As you browse through this library you will find several years of outreach influence team meeting agendas, samples of level 3 to level 4 influence plans, an outreach influence team leader ministry description, training and informational videos, and more. We are constantly updating and adding to these tools, so check back often.

You can contact the OOI team through the website (www .OrganicOutreach.org) or by email (info@OrganicOutreach.org).

Organic Outreach International is a ministry of Shoreline Community Church in Monterey, California.

Simple, Natural Ways to Share Your Faith

Organic Outreach for Churches DVD	9780310537694	$29.99
Organic Outreach for Ordinary People DVD	9780310531197	$29.99
Organic OutreachforOrdinaryPeopleBook	9780310566106	$16.99
Organic Outreach for Churches Book	9780310566076	$16.99
Organic Outreach for Families Book	9780310273974	$16.99

ZONDERVAN®